CYCLING
IN SCOTLAND

John Hancox

HarperCollins*Publishers*

First published 1997

Reprint 10 9 8 7 6 5 4 3 2 1 0

© Text, John Hancox, 1997
© Maps, Bartholomews, 1997
Reproduced by kind permission of HarperCollins*Cartographic*

Cover photograph: View towards Ben Lomond from Creag-Ard House, Milton, near Aberfoyle (© Graham Lees)

ISBN 0 00 471010-X

A catalogue record for this book is available from the British Library

Reference Department
HarperCollins*Publishers*
PO Box
Glasgow G4 0NB

Origination by Arneg Limited, Glasgow
Printed in Italy by Rotolito Lombarda S.p.A.

CONTENTS

HOW TO USE THIS BOOK

Cycling in Scotland is a clear and comprehensive guide to touring routes and shorter excursions throughout this beautiful and varied country. The wiro binding enables the pages to be folded completely back on themselves, keeping the appropriate page to view, without the travelling cyclist having to hold the book open.

The main body of *Cycling in Scotland* is divided into 11 chapters, each covering a different part of the country and all arranged in a similar manner. Each chapter contains:

1. *An overview fact sheet.* This gives details on the routes in the chapter, with their difficulty levels and distances, plus general information on public transport, tourist offices which are open all year round and special events.

2. *A Grand Tour route description.* Starting and finishing at Gretna on the border with England north of Carlisle, the Grand Tour winds through the whole of mainland Scotland, as well as taking in Arran and the Western Isles. The first excursion described in chapters 1, 2, 3, 6, 7, 8 and 9 is a part of the Grand Tour, which in total is a distance of about 1000 miles. It is estimated that a reasonably fit cyclist should take 3-4 weeks to complete the whole route.

3. *A selection of shorter routes within each area.* These routes vary in difficulty from Easy to Strenuous, and all, including the Grand Tour, have route direction and distance information, plus visitor attractions, places of interest, accommodation and eating establishments highlighted along the way.

4. *Specific fact sheets.* Each excursion has a more detailed fact sheet, which includes information on which Ordnance Survey 1:50,000 maps to use, plus smaller tourist offices, cycle shops, hostels, banks and launderettes along or near the route. NOTE: The information in some fact sheets is relevant to more than one excursion.

5. *Route maps.* Comprehensive and up-to-date Bartholomews 1:250,000 (1 inch = 4 miles) maps are used throughout the book as base mapping on which the various cycling tours have been superimposed as a purple dotted line. In the case of the Grand Tour, there is generally more than one page of mapping for each part of the overall route. NOTE: More than one excursion appears on certain maps. Cross-references to the appropriate maps are to be found in the excursion texts.

6. *Historical/cultural features.* These short résumés on Scottish subjects ranging from Robert Burns to Malt Whisky and from Covenanters to Harris Tweed are scattered throughout the book. Each is highlighted by a blue panel behind the heading and there are also cross-references within the text.

At the back of the book you will find a series of appendices, with sections on planning a cycling holiday, mountain biking and official long-distance cycling routes, plus a map indicating the start and finish points of each stage of the Grand Tour. A full index and pages for making notes complete this invaluable guide, which no touring cyclist in Scotland will want to be without.

Key to Route Difficulty

♦	Easy
♦ (♦)	Easy to moderate
♦♦	Moderate
♦♦ (♦)	Moderate to strenuous
♦♦♦	Strenuous

Difficulty indicators appear in the fact sheet at the beginning of each chapter, as well as alongside the heading for each route.

INTRODUCTION

Cycling in Scotland is all about variety. From the rugged grandeur of the West Coast to the soft, fertile Borders, there is just about everything a cyclist could wish for. Huge empty beaches with magical turquoise water welcome you in the Western Isles, while the quiet roads and picturesque fishing villages of Fife have a special atmosphere all of their own.

From a cycling standpoint, Scotland ranges from the sublime to the ridiculous. Some routes are very challenging and remote, and extremely rewarding provided you are fit enough and well prepared. Other areas are better if you want a relaxed holiday pottering around. I have tried to vary routes to provide satisfying options for different tastes. Some people may regard 20 miles as a long day, while others will cruise through 120 miles.

This book has been devised to cater for all levels of fitness and experience. For the fit and more ambitious there is the 'Grand Tour of Scotland' – taking three to four weeks – travelling through the very best parts of this wonderful country. Based on this route, and covering all parts of Scotland, are moderate and easy loops and mountain bike routes, giving more flexibility. Due to the less than ideal provision of public transport, mountain bike routes, and moderate and easy loops suitable for weekends or family trips, sometimes rely on taking a car to the starting point.

It is strange how many people come to Scotland to cycle and never unload their bikes. Driving around with a bike on the roof is not (absolutely not) a cycling holiday, despite what many people say. There is a barrier to getting started but when you do get going cycling rewards you by making you fitter and providing wonderful opportunities to see Scotland's rich wildlife at close quarters. Gliding silently along on a bike, you inevitably see deer, heron and eagles, and you may be lucky enough to find otters. There is also the rich aroma of gorse and other wild flowers, and the wind whistling through your hair, which you just have to experience.

Cycling gives visitors to Scotland a much better feel for the landscape than touring about in a car. You move slower and stop more often to enjoy the view, but you can still cover good distances. Scotland is also a wonderful place for mountain biking, with large networks of hill roads, drove roads and forestry tracks opening up the wildest and most inaccessible areas. But caution is essential in wild areas, and cyclists should only go with good maps, plenty of food, appropriate equipment and sufficient experience to be able to cope with what can be a harsh climate even in the middle of summer.

Public access to Scotland's hills is by tradition allowed by landowners and respected by walkers and cyclists. There is no penalty for trespass provided damage or nuisance is not caused. Generally the legal position is that, as bicycles are human-powered, cyclists have the same rights as walkers in terms of rights of way. If in doubt, ask at estate offices or farms about access and camping. Most importantly, ask permission during the lambing season (April and May), grouse-shooting season (12 August-October) and the deer season (August to mid-October). A useful guide is *Heading for the Scottish Hills*, published by the Mountaineering Council of Scotland, which lists who owns what. Generally, folk who work in estate offices are helpful.

Do not be fooled into thinking that cycling is particularly cheap. A good rule is to take half as many belongings (i.e. clothes, books, etc.) as you think you will need and twice as much money. And take the money in cash. That way you won't have anxious detours looking for a bank.

The best time to visit Scotland seems to be May-early June and September-October. The weather at these times tends to be more settled but rather cooler than high summer. Often the middle of summer is cloudier, and the West Coast in particular is prone to midges. The Scottish winter can be wonderful but many tourist facilities close down from November to Easter.

Good cycling!

THE SOUTHWEST

This underestimated and largely unexplored part of Scotland is a real gem, often missed by tourists stampeding north. It is fairly flat, farming is prevalent and there are beautiful forests, although the area doesn't have the rugged grandeur of the northern Highlands. It is ideal for a relaxed holiday pottering around by bicycle, as there are countless quiet roads and many beautiful little towns. The high density of towns and villages means you are never too far from cafés or bike shops.

➤ **Route 1 (Grand Tour)**
   Gretna-Dumfries-Cumnock-Ardrossan
   ♦♦ Moderate, with some hills. 104 miles.

➤ **Route 2**
   Smugglers' Road Loop: Dumfries-Gatehouse of Fleet
   ♦♦ Moderate. 90 miles.

➤ **Route 3**
   Dumfries-Caerlaverock
   ♦ Easy. 24 miles.

➤ **Route 4**
   Off-road loop from Newton Stewart
   ♦♦ Moderate mountain bike route. 36 miles.

➤ **Rail**
   Rail access is relatively good, with stations at Dumfries, Sanquhar and Stranraer. Dumfries and Sanquhar are on the Carlisle-Glasgow line and Stranraer can be reached from Glasgow Central. Tel. 0345 484950 (enquiries) and 0345 550033 (bookings).

➤ **Ferries**
   Stranraer-Belfast/Larne, Northern Ireland
   Seacat Terminal, Stranraer, tel. 0345 523523
   Cairnryan-Larne, Northern Ireland
   P&O European Ferries, Cairnryan, tel. 01581 200276
   Stranraer-Belfast, Northern Ireland
   Stena Sealink Travel Centre, Sealink Terminal, Stranraer, tel. 01776 702262

➤ **Cycle Tour Organizers**
   Roundabout Scotland, 4 Observatory Lane, Glasgow G12 9AH,
   tel. 0141 337-3877

➤ **Tourist Information Offices (Open all year)**
   Ayr, 39 Sandgate, tel. 01292 288688
   Dumfries, Whitesands, tel. 01387 253862
   Gretna, Gateway to Scotland, M74 Service Area, tel. 01461 338500
   Mauchline, National Burns Memorial, tel. 01290 551916

➤ **Special Events**
   Dumfries has a Burns Festival Week in September and Sanquhar has the
   Riding of the Marches in July.

GRAND TOUR

Route 1: Gretna-Dumfries-Cumnock-Ardrossan

See Fact Sheets 1 and 2

Stage 1: Gretna-Dumfries

A demanding route for leaner, keener cycle tourists. This is the first
part of the Grand Tour of Scotland, heading for Ardrossan and on to
Arran and the West Coast. This is the route to take to avoid the
worst of the urban Central Belt of Scotland, with its busy roads. The
area around Irvine requires care, but there is a signposted cycle route
off-road and on quieter roads.

Gretna is a small border town, its fame for marriages dating from the
time following the 1754 Hardwicke Marriage Act, which forced lovers
to flee across the border from England to Scotland where the marriage laws were less strict. This continued even into the 20thC, as
age of consent rules in Scotland differed. The idea that the marriage
should be conducted by a blacksmith dates from the fact that Joseph
Paisley, the Gretna blacksmith, conducted these ceremonies between
1791 and 1814. There is a museum in the smithy now, and also a
Sunday market at the west side of the town.

Head west on the B721 along the coast. Continue through Annan, a
reasonable sized town. Avoid the busy A75.

Carry on along the pleasant but fairly uneventful back roads past
Caerlaverock Castle, with its bird reserve, before looping north into
Dumfries. Caerlaverock ('Lark's nest') Castle is now a very fine ruin

which was seized by Edward I of England in 1300. It had a Renaissance-style façade added in the 17thC. (Admission charge.) The Wildfowl and Wetlands Centre near Bankend is a nature reserve where the barnacle geese from Spitzbergen are a great conservation success story, although the farmers don't like them as they graze on fields. The geese winter here and leave in April. (Admission charge.)

The area around Dumfries is very quiet, with rolling hills and large forests. Nearer the Solway coast the terrain is very flat with plenty of little roads. As you head north the terrain gets more hilly. It is a wonderfully undiscovered part of Scotland, generally missed by people travelling north. It enjoys one of the best climates in the country, although you shouldn't bank on it.   ➤ 15

Fact Sheet 1 . . . .

Dumfries & Gretna

Dumfries and Gretna are fairly busy towns, and both have a number of historical associations. Cycling along the Solway coast is rewarding, and not too hilly, but there is a good deal of traffic on the main roads. Dumfries is famous as the home of Robert Burns, Scotland's best-known poet.

➤ **OS Maps 84, 85**

➤ **Tourist Information Offices (Summer only)**
Gretna Green, Old Blacksmith's Shop, tel. 01461 337834
Southwaite, M6 Service Area Northbound, Cumbria, tel. 01697 473445

➤ **Cycle Shops**
Kirkpatrick Cycles, 13-15 Queen Street, Dumfries, tel. 01387 254011
Nithdale Cycles, Brooms Road, Dumfries, tel. 01387 254870
Grierson & Graham, 10 Academy Street, Dumfries, tel. 01387 259483

➤ **Hostels**
There are no SYHA or other hostels in the area.

➤ **Banks**
These are plentiful. There are three in both Dumfries and Annan, and one in Gretna.

➤ **Launderettes**
26 Annan Road, Dumfries, tel. 01387 252295
52 Lincluden Road, Dumfries, tel. 01387 261825

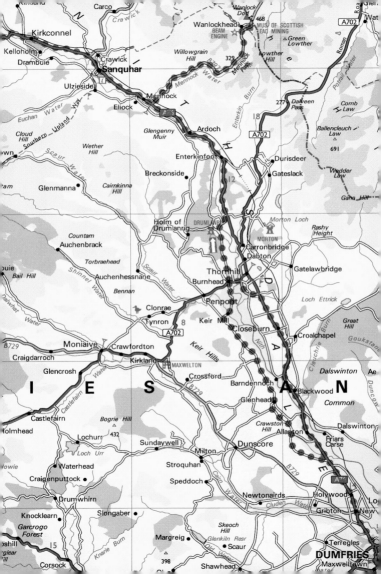

Ayrshire

Ayr, Irvine, Kilmarnock and the surrounding area are largely residential and industrial, and are only of passing interest to visitors doing the Grand Tour. It is best to take a ferry to Arran.

➤ **OS Maps 70, 76, 77**

➤ **Tourist Information Offices (Summer only)**
Ardrossan, Ferry Terminal, The Harbour, tel. 01294 601063
Girvan, Bridge Street, tel. 01465 714950
Kilmarnock, 62 Bank Street, tel. 01563 539090
Sanquhar, The Tolbooth, High Street, tel. 01659 50185
Troon, South Beach, tel. 01292 317686

➤ **Rail**
Access is good, as Strathclyde Passenger Transport Executive (SPTE) permits bikes on trains free, providing there is room. Tel. 0345 212282 for further information. There are regular services to Ayr and Kilmarnock.

➤ **Ferry**
Ardrossan-Brodick, Arran.
There is a Tourist Information Desk on the ship.
Caledonian MacBrayne, tel. 01475 650100

➤ **Cycle Shops**
Carrick Cycles, 87 Main Street, Ayr, tel. 01292 269822
Carrick Cycles, 126 Dalrymple Street, Girvan, tel. 01465 714189.
The proprietors of Carrick Cycles are working on waymarked cycle routes in the area. Ask at the shops for details.
Kilmarnock Cycles, High Glencairn Street, Kilmarnock, tel. 01563 538938
Irvine Cycles, Eglinton Street, Irvine, tel. 01294 272712
Davidson Sports, Forum Centre, Irvine, tel. 01294 313332
AMG Cycles, Hamilton Street, Saltcoats, tel. 01294 463421

➤ **Hostels**
SYHA, Ayr, Craigwell Road, tel. 01292 262322
SYHA, Wanlockhead, near Biggar, tel. 01659 74387

➤ **Banks**
These, and other services, are plentiful in the area.

➤ **Launderettes**
At Ayr SYHA (see above)

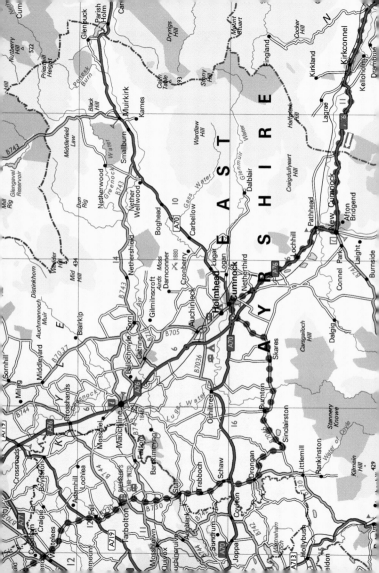

Dumfries and Galloway is renowned for its links with famous literary figures, such as Robert Burns (see feature on page 16) and Thomas Carlyle (1795-1881), historian and sage, who was born in Ecclefechan and educated in Annan.

Stage 2: Dumfries-Cumnock

There are two alternative routes north of Dumfries. Either take the A76 along the River Nith to Thornhill, or turn left about 5 miles north of Dumfries onto quiet back roads to the west of the river. Either way, just north of Thornhill you should visit the impressive Drumlanrig Castle and the museum celebrating Kirkpatrick MacMillan (see bicycle feature on page 17). The grounds form part of the estate of the Duke of Buccleuch, one of Scotland's richest landowners, and are quite remarkable, with some really beautiful trees. The castle is open to the public and has important artworks and a magnificent silver chandelier. There is also a bedroom where Bonnie Prince Charlie slept. If you just visit the castle, bikes can be hired to use around the estate, and there are also craft shops and a café. (Admission charge.)

The countryside consists of pleasant rolling hills, and despite being a main road the A76 is not too busy. The journey can be broken by stopping at the small hostel at Wanlockhead, on the hilly B797. To be honest, this is for really tough cyclists. Wanlockhead is the highest village in Scotland and getting there involves a 6 mile climb to 1530 ft. The Leadmining Museum, tel. 01659 74387, is worth a visit. (Admission charge.) As well as leadmining, gold extracted here was used in the 16thC Scottish crown and regalia, which are now on display in Edinburgh Castle. More recently, international gold panners have arrived who can occasionally be seen standing in burns swirling gravel.

Mining has also affected Cumnock, the town where the River Glaisnock meets the Lugar Water. Cumnock was the home of Keir Hardie in the 1880s. He was a miners' leader and caused a sensation by wearing a cloth cap and tweeds, when he was in parliament as an MP for the Independent Labour Party.

Stage 3: Cumnock-Ardrossan

The main road between Kilmarnock and Irvine is a dual carriageway and best avoided.

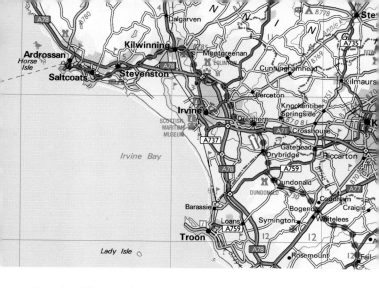

The advisable route from Cumnock is to take the B7046 and B730 north through Tarbolton before bypassing Irvine to the east and join-ing the A737 to Kilwinning and on to Ardrossan. There are plenty of little back roads to explore, but the assumption is that you will bash on to the ferry at Ardrossan to continue the Grand Tour.

If you decide to take the B741 from New Cumnock towards the coast at Girvan, you will be near the scene where many incendiary bombs were washed ashore after being disturbed. This led to the revelation in 1995 that the MOD had dumped by hand millions of tonnes of spent munitions left over from World War II. Despite the fact that they were 'spent', there has been a history of explosions measurable by seismic equipment.

ROBERT BURNS

Robert Burns (1759-96), 'Scotland's national bard', is well-known internationally for his poetry and songs, including *My Love is like a Red, Red Rose* and *Auld Lang Syne*. He was born on a small farm in Alloway, near Ayr, the land of which had to support a family of seven children; Robert was the eldest. As was common in Scotland, education was considered important, even in poor families, and the Burns children were educated by their father.

Robert started writing songs and poems when he was 14 and by his mid-20s was an accomplished writer. In 1786 he had his first book of poems published in Kilmarnock. *Poems, Chiefly in the Scottish Dialect* was received with critical acclaim and the 'Ploughman Poet' was enthusiastically welcomed into Edinburgh's literary society. He travelled extensively throughout Scotland, collecting poetry and writings, and returned to Ayr in 1788 to marry Jean Armour, with whom he already had a family. He then took a farm at Ellisland, near Dumfries, and wrote two of his most famous works, *Tam o' Shanter* and *Auld Lang Syne*. He died at the age of 37.

Often thought of as a womanizer and drinker, Burns in fact captured in his poems the rhythm of the Scots language, and his sense of human worth and ideas of equality and liberty marked him out as a revolutionary. So controversial were his ideas that he published some of his work anonymously, protecting his job as a civil servant and keeping generations of academics in work. Burns' birthday, 25 January, is marked by Burns Suppers worldwide, at which haggis is eaten then washed down with whisky.

Burns enthusiasts visiting Dumfries can see Ellisland Farm, 6 miles north on the A6, while in the centre of town are his drinking haunts, the King's Arms and Globe Hotel, plus a Burns House and Robert Burns Centre (admission charge). In Alloway are the Burns Cottage and Museum (admission charge), the Land o' Burns Visitor Centre (free) and the Brig o' Doon.

THE BICYCLE

The area around Dumfries is a place of pilgrimage for the enthusiastic cyclist, as it was here in 1846 that the bicycle was invented by Kirkpatrick Macmillan, a blacksmith of Couthill in Dumfries. Macmillan made it possible to preserve a continuity of motion on a balanced vehicle without touching the ground with the feet. Though the first two-wheeled vehicle had been made in France as early as 1808, it was propelled by the feet. Macmillan's stroke of genius was in fixing cranks connected to long levers to the rear wheels, making it possible to ride a two-wheeled single-track vehicle. Sadly, Macmillan's fame was posthumous, as the bicycle he was riding knocked down a child. He was prosecuted within weeks of the invention, which was promptly suppressed for the next fifty years.

The smithy at Couthill where the first bike was built still exists, although it is not a tourist attraction. There is, however, a museum at Drumlanrig Castle, tel. 01848 331555/330248, 18 miles north of Dumfries, which has early bicycles celebrating the inventor. (Admission charge for castle: museum by donation.) There are some easy cycling routes through the Drumlanrig estate, which are particularly suitable for families.

Route 2: Smugglers' Road Loop: Dumfries-Gatehouse of Fleet-Dumfries

◆ See Fact Sheets 1 and 3

In the 17th and 18thC, this coast proved ideal for the smuggling of spirits and silks from France and Spain via the Isle of Man, thereby evading English taxes.

From Dumfries railway station, head into town and follow the Solway Coast and Dalbeattie signs across the River Nith. Take the A710 to New Abbey and enjoy an easy 8 mile meander. Sweetheart Abbey is so-called because it was founded in 1273 by Devorguilla Balliol, who died with the heart of her dead husband in her arms. She also founded a hostel in Oxford which became Balliol College. (Admission charge.) The Crieffel Inn, New Abbey, tel. 01387 850305, does good bar meals and has accommodation. Another attraction is Shambellie House Museum of Costume, which has displays from the national costume collection. (Admission charge.) It's also worth taking a look at the old working corn mill. Continue to Dalbeattie, with good views of the Solway. In winter rare barnacle geese from Spitzbergen in the Arctic Ocean feed on the salt marshes, as well as on farmers' fields. In summer, there is a good variety of birdlife.

Branch off down the coast 3 miles past New Abbey to Arbigland Gardens, which overlook the Nith estuary. There is a cottage here where John Paul Jones was born in 1747. He fought in the American Wars of Independence and founded the US Navy. (Admission charge.)

Fact Sheet 3 . . . . **West Galloway**

West Galloway is particularly good cycling country, with plenty of quiet back roads and interesting towns and villages. It is therefore a pity that many visitors miss this area. Keen cyclists will find opportunities for mountain biking in the extensive forests.

➤ **OS Maps 76, 77, 82, 83**

➤ **Tourist Information Offices (Summer only)**
Castle Douglas, Market Hill Car Park, tel. 01556 502611
Dalbeattie, Town Hall, tel. 01556 610177
Gatehouse of Fleet, The Square, tel. 01557 814212
Kirkcudbright, Harbour Square, tel. 01557 330494
Newton Stewart, Dashwood Square, tel. 01671 402431
Stranraer, 1 Bridge Street, tel. 01776 702595

➤ **Cycle Shops**
Ace Cycles, Church Street, Castle Douglas, tel. 01556 504542
W. Law, St Cuthbert Street, Kirkcudbright, tel. 01557 330579
R.S. Bowie, Queen Street, Stranraer, tel. 01776 702836
Carrick Cycles, King Street, Stranraer, tel. 01776 889515

➤ **Hostels**
SYHA, Minnigaff, near Newton Stewart, tel. 01671 402211
SYHA, Kendoon, near St John's Town of Dalry, north of New Galloway.
No telephone.

➤ **Banks**
There are banks in most of the towns in this area, including Stranraer, Kirkcudbright and Newton Stewart.

➤ **Mountain Biking**
For details of forest trails, contact the Forestry Commission offices at Creebridge, tel. 01671 402420, Newton Stewart, tel. 01556 503626, or Ae Forest, tel. 01387 860247.

The coast road makes a very pleasant cycle with no significant hills. There is a National Trust nature reserve at Rockcliffe on nearby Rough Island. Dalbeattie is famous for its granite, which was used to build the Eddystone Lighthouse and the Thames Embankment. The Maxwell Arms Hotel, tel. 01556 610431, has good food.   ➤ 22

Between Dalbeattie and Kirkcudbright the route goes past Orchardton Tower, a rather elegant 15thC tower house, and Dundrennan Abbey, now a magnificent ruin, where Mary Queen of Scots stopped off on her way to nearby Port Mary on her ill-fated journey to England. (Admission charges.) There are many tracks and small roads down to the coast, giving plenty of opportunities for exploration.

Kirkcudbright is a cheerful little town with an attractive fishing harbour, and has long been a magnet for artists. The Stewartry Museum, tel. 01557 331643, documents local history and has a fine art collection, including work by Jessie M. King, a successful exponent of the Glasgow Style at the turn of the century. (Admission charge.) The Solway Coast Tearoom in St Mary Street serves excellent evening meals, while the Mill on the Fleet has a restored bobbin mill with excellent displays and a great tearoom.

Take the A755 out of Kirkcudbright, signposted to Gatehouse of Fleet. It is a fairly long, slow and painful climb out of town but it gets easier after a while. Natural hazards abound, in the form of cows in the road, as well as stray sheep, tractors and mud.

Join the A75 and cross over to detour into Gatehouse of Fleet. It's a pleasant cycle through Cally Forest and down into the carefully preserved town. There's good food at the Murray Arms Hotel, and also the Masonic Arms by the clock tower.

Head north on a minor road via Darngarroch to Laurieston, before taking the B795 to Townhead of Greenlaw and turning south through Castle Douglas to Threave Garden, tel. 01556 502575, which is most famous for its daffodils in spring, as well as its rhododendrons, and is managed by students. (Admission charge.)

Return through Castle Douglas and take the minor road to Haugh of Urr. This quiet old military road, which rolls through farmland, avoids the busy A75. Branch off left to Crocketford, also known as Ninemile Bar, if you need refreshments. At Lochfoot the lochan has the visible remains of a crannog, a Neolithic lake dwelling. From here it is just a few miles back into Dumfries.

Route 3:
Dumfries-Caerlaverock Castle-Dumfries
See Fact Sheet 1 and first Map for Route 1

Dumfries is the oldest burgh in the southwest, created in 1186. At the friary which once stood opposite the present-day Greyfriars Church, Robert the Bruce murdered John Comyn, his rival for the Scottish throne, in 1306. The Old Bridge Museum, in a building dating back to 1660, has re-creations of a Victorian nursery and dental laboratory. (Admission charge.)

This is a gentle ride, heading south from Dumfries along the B725 beside the Nith estuary towards Caerlaverock Castle, tel. 01387 770244. (Admission charge.) The castle is described in Route 1. Behind it is a small hill which has the remains of a Roman fort, and there are picnic places in the carefully tended grounds. Nearby is the Wildfowl and Wetlands Centre, a good place for birdwatching, described in Route 1. (Admission charge.) Complete this short loop by continuing on the B725 to Bankend and heading back into Dumfries.

Route 4: Off-road loop from Newton Stewart
See Fact Sheet 3

This is a very satisfying round trip through varied scenery. Part of the route is on the Southern Upland Way, where walkers have priority. Returning from Glen Trool, you pass through the Wood of Cree, one of the finest oak and birch woodlands in the country, which is now a nature reserve. There are beautiful forest flowers in April and May.

From Minnigaff Hostel near Newton Stewart travel northeast on the A712 for about 13 miles. At Clatteringshaws Loch there is a Forestry Commission tearoom, as well as wildlife exhibits such as swooping eagles. (Free.) Head west on forest tracks. OS map 77 is helpful. Pass the Black Water of Dee, a very pleasant river, and join up with the Southern Upland Way. There's a bothy on the south side of Loch Dee where you can camp for free. The track now gets quite rough and

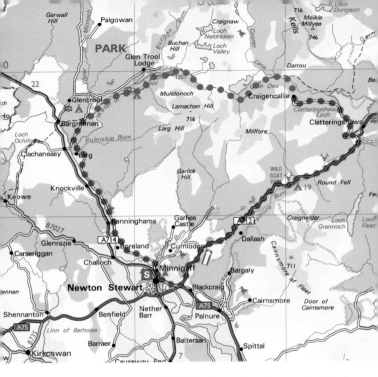

cycling is not always possible. Take the track to the south of Loch Trool. The loch is famed for a skirmish in 1306 when Robert the Bruce rolled boulders onto his English foes. The Martyrs' Tomb is a memorial to six covenanters (see feature on page 25) who were killed while at prayer nearby in 1685. Return along the east bank of the River Cree on lovely quiet roads to Newton Stewart.

This area is crisscrossed by tracks which are good to explore by mountain bike. Some of these are newly created by the Forestry Commission; others are ancient, and were originally old drovers' roads. The area was fiercely fought over during the Civil War which raged in the 17thC. The justification was religious, but the true motive seems to involve cattle being seized and carried off to Gretna, which was then bandit country and claimed by England.

COVENANTERS

During the reign of Charles I (1625-49) an attempt was made to make Scotland conform to the religious principles and practice of England with the re-introduction of bishops and the 1637 *Book of Common Prayer*. In 1638 the National Covenant was drawn up and signed in Edinburgh, and eventually there were 300,000 signatories, all committed to the independence of the Church from the king. However, the Covenanters became divided once Civil War broke out in England. Covenanters who left the Church in protest against the link between Church and state to worship in 'conventicles' or meeting houses were persecuted. It was a period of religious fanaticism which was suppressed by military means. The bloodiest phase, known as the 'Killing Times', occurred in the 1680s after the restoration of Charles II, who again introduced episcopalianism, having been forced to sign the Covenant by Oliver Cromwell. After the death of Charles II the debate continued as a political and religious issue, and eventually led to the formation of the Free Church in 1876.

ARRAN, KINTYRE, ISLAY & JURA

This area is little short of a miracle. Only a couple of hours by public transport from Glasgow and you can be on Arran, Bute or the lovely Cowal Peninsula. This region has that marvellous slow-moving island feel, and the views from the Mull of Kintyre plus the many Celtic remains make it extra special. The loop routes described in this chapter are ideal for a weekend or as part of a leisurely holiday. The area is easily accessible from the Scottish Central Belt, with many trains operating to both the north and south Clyde coasts, plus a comprehensive ferry service to islands in the Firth of Clyde and beyond Kintyre. However, the railway service to and from Oban is somewhat infrequent.

➤ **Route 5 (Grand Tour)**
Round Arran
♦♦ Moderate, with some hills. 56 miles for full circuit.

➤ **Route 6**
North Arran
♦♦ Moderate, with one quite strenuous hill climb. 17 miles.

➤ **Route 7 (Grand Tour)**
Claonaig-Lochgilphead-Oban
♦♦ Moderate to strenuous, with rolling hills. 80 miles.

➤ **Route 8**
Islay & Jura
♦ Easy. 154 miles.

➤ **Route 9**
Cowal Peninsula
♦♦ Moderate, with some hills. 48 miles.

➤ **Route 10**
Rothesay & the Kyles of Bute
♦ Easy, with some small hills. 49 miles.

➤ **Route 11**
Round Great Cumbrae
♦ Easy. 10 miles.

➤ **Rail**
There are frequent rail services from Glasgow Central to Largs, Ardrossan and Wemyss Bay, plus services from Glasgow Queen Street to Helensburgh and Oban. Tel. 0345 484950 (enquiries) or 0345 550033 (bookings).

➤ **Ferries**

Caledonian Macbrayne operates ferries to Arran, Bute and Cumbrae in the Clyde estuary, plus from Kintyre to Islay and Jura, between Arran and Kintyre and the Cowal Peninsula and Kintyre, and from Gourock to Dunoon across the Clyde. For more information, contact Caledonian Macbrayne, tel. 01475 650100.

➤ **Tourist Information Offices (Open all year)**

Bowmore, Islay, tel. 01496 810254
Brodick, Arran, The Pier, tel. 01770 302401
Dunoon, 7 Alexandra Parade, tel. 01369 703785
Oban, Argyll Square, tel. 01631 563122
Rothesay, Bute, 15 Victoria Street, tel. 01700 502151

➤ **Clyde Tour Organizers**

Bespoke Highland Tours, The Bothy, Camusdarroch by Arisaig, Inverness-shire, tel. 0141 334-9017 or 01687 450272
Scottish Youth Hostels Association Island-hopping Holidays to Arran and Islay. Contact 7 Glebe Crescent, Stirling, tel. 01786 451181

➤ **Special Events**

The area is famous for its Highland Games, particularly those held on Arran and in Dunoon (the Cowal Highland Gathering) in August. The Islay Festival takes place in late May/early June, the Arran Folk Festival in June and the Bute Folk Festival in late July.

GRAND TOUR
Route 5: Round Arran

See Fact Sheet 4

Arran is one of the most accessible West Coast islands, and it's certainly worth spending time on. It is said that the island represents Scotland in miniature. The craggy peaks of Goat Fell to the north and the fertile land in the south tend to confirm this. Its circumnavigation makes for a long day, and there are some quite steep hills between Brodick and Whiting Bay, made tougher if the wind is strong. However, there is a short cut, The String Road, from Blackwaterfoot to Brodick which is also over a big hill, but which cuts off about 15

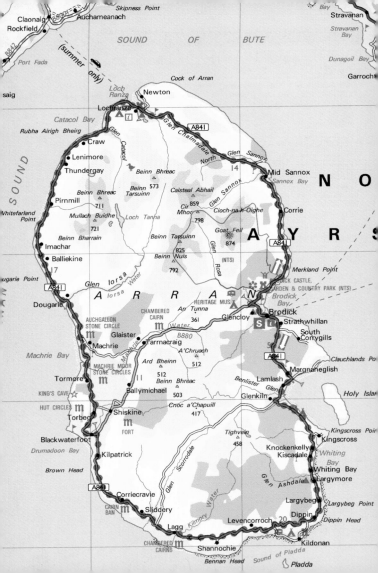

miles. It is possible to cycle round the island in a normal day during the summer, arriving at Brodick about 9 am and being on the ferry home at 7 pm. There is only one mountain bike track, courtesy of the Forestry Commission, between Lamlash and Kilmory via Glenashdale (see OS map 69). Others are due to open; ask bike shops for details.

Brodick is the main centre of Arran, and has various interesting tourist attractions, including the Arran Heritage Museum Brodick Castle is a National Trust property and ancient seat of the Dukes of Hamilton. It contains superb silver, porcelain and paintings. There are formal and informal gardens, plus woodland walks among a magnificent collection of trees, which includes the rare Arran Whitebeam. There is also an excellent tearoom. (Admission charge.)

At Lamlash is Holy Isle which has been bought by the Samye Ling Monastery in Dumfries and Galloway as a place of retreat. The road to Whiting Bay and round the south end of Arran is quite hilly and you'll be grateful for the comfortable armchairs of the Lagg Hotel.

Arran's west coast has great views of Kintyre, and is served by more teashops than any other island I know, which is of fundamental importance if you are not desperately fit. Round the island, ideal stops are the golf club at Corrie, the Pier Café, Lamlash and the Lagg Hotel, which serves bar lunches and afternoon teas. Much of Arran is quiet, peaceful and pretty wild, although there is a slight twee-ness to some of the more tourist-oriented parts. However, Arran Aromatics and the Island Cheese Shop have quality locally produced gifts for sale at Brodick Home Farm, tel. 01770 302788.

At Machrie Moor there are six Neolithic standing stones. Also nearby is the cave by Drumadoon Point, Blackwaterfoot, where Robert the Bruce supposedly had his famous encounter with a spider. As you continue along this coast it is possible to see many wading birds and often seals.

For details of attractions in the north of Arran between Lochranza and Brodick, see Route 6.

Fact Sheet 4 ....

Arran

Arran is suitable for relaxed weekend cycling, helped by the provision of plentiful tourist facilities. In summer it can get very busy with tourists, so booking ahead is advisable. However, the island in general has very light traffic, and the varied scenery makes it a rewarding experience. There are some hills to cycle up, and many midges in summer.

➤ **OS Map 69**

➤ **Tourist Information Office (Summer only)**
   Lochranza, tel. 01770 700339

➤ **Rail**
   There are regular trains from Glasgow Central to Ardrossan, some connecting directly with the ferry to Brodick.

➤ **Ferry**
   Ardrossan-Brodick/Brodick-Rothesay/Lochranza-Claonaig, Kintyre.
   There is a Tourist Information Desk on the Ardrossan-Brodick ship.
   Caledonian Macbrayne, tel. 01475 650100

➤ **Cycle Shops**
   Mini Golf Cycle Hire, Brodick, tel. 01770 302272
   Brodick Cycles, tel. 01770 302460
   Whiting Bay Cycle Hire, tel. 01770 700382
   Spinning Wheels, Corrie, tel. 01770 810640

➤ **Hostels**
   SYHA, Lochranza, tel. 01770 830631
   SYHA, Whiting Bay, tel. 01770 700339

➤ **Banks**
   Brodick, Royal Bank of Scotland, tel. 01770 302222.
   Mobile unit elsewhere on the island.

➤ **Mountain Biking**
   Leaflets are available from bike shops or the Forestry Commission, tel. 01770 302218, for an off-road route from Lamlash to Kilmory.

Route 6: North Arran

See Fact Sheet 4 and Map for Route 5

North of Brodick, Goat Fell (2866 ft) and Caisteal Abhail rise spectacularly and are still snow-tipped in spring.

The road that follows Arran's east shore is delightful. The little cottages have roses and flower gardens, and ducks and geese waddle down by the waterside. When the gorse bushes are in bloom, there is a coconut-like scent everywhere. There are plenty of hotels and pubs that serve teas or meals to hungry cyclists, and the Corrie Hotel can be recommended. After Corrie the road leaves the shore and climbs steeply, leaving the pretty woodlands behind. The hill up Glen Sannox is by no means the worst in these parts, but the surrounding moorland feels more like wilderness for being so near to Glasgow. Lochranza Castle is a picturesque ruin which was originally built in the 13th-14thC. On my visit I stayed at Lochranza Youth Hostel, busy with college groups finishing term, so I wandered along to a pub, past Lochranza Castle, and sat outside watching the sun sinking over Kintyre. Inside the bar an accordion and a mouth organ had appeared, and everyone was set for a party, which was getting quite lively by the time I headed reluctantly back to the hostel in time for curfew.

GRAND TOUR
Route 7: Claonaig-Lochgilphead-Oban

See Fact Sheet 5

This section starts at the tiny Claonaig pier where the Arran ferry arrives from Lochranza. The cycle over to Tarbert is easy, passing through some lovely birch woods. The main road (A83) which runs up through Kintyre is quiet apart from some lorries carrying timber from the huge forestry plantations here. The road is OK for cycling, although loop roads off to the west past Kilmory and Kilberry allow quiet detours through lovely scenery. North of Lochgilphead are some strenuous hills which give amazing views and great freewheeling on the way down. However, the hills make this a long 60 mile run. ➤ 33

Oban & Kintyre

Oban is known as the Gateway to the Isles. As a railhead and as a centre for Caledonian Macbrayne ferries, the town is often passed through. It is a snug, friendly town, with plenty to do, if you find the peace and quiet of island life is getting too much. People travel for days to get a curry! There are some mountain biking routes locally and quiet roads east through Glen Lonan, or south to Seil Island and Luing. The area around Kilmartin has amazing prehistoric and Celtic remains, as well as fantastic scenery.

➤ **OS Map 49**

➤ **Tourist Information Offices (Summer only)**
Lochgilphead, Lochnell Street, tel. 01546 602344
Tarbert, Harbour Street, tel. 01880 820429

➤ **Rail**
There are generally 3-4 trains per day from Glasgow Queen Street to Oban, via Crianlarich. Book bike accommodation in advance.

➤ **Ferries**
Ferries operate from Oban to Mull, Barra, South Uist, Colonsay, Lismore, Kerrera, Tiree and Islay, and from Kennacraig to Islay and Jura.
Caledonian Macbrayne, tel. 01475 650100

➤ **Cycle Shops**
Oban Cycles, 9 Craigard Road, tel. 01631 566996/563420. Mountain bike hire and spares. The enthusiastic and helpful staff get my vote.
David Graham, 9 Combie Street, Oban, tel. 01631 562069
Leitch, Tarbert, Kintyre, tel. 01880 820287. Bike hire and limited repairs. It is also a launderette!
Crinan Cycles, Unit 6, Pier Square, Ardrishaig, tel. 01546 603511

➤ **Hostels**
SYHA, Oban, tel. 01631 562025. Grade 1, with a washing machine.
Jeremy Inglis Independent Hostel, 21 Airds Crescent, Oban, tel. 01631 563064
Accommodation en route:
Cuilfail Hotel, by Loch Melfort, tel. 01852 200274
Kilmartin Hotel, Kilmartin, tel. 01546 510250. Friendly pub with open fires.
Tigh-na-Truish, Clachan, Isle of Seil, tel. 01852 300242. A slight detour but a fantastic setting next to the Bridge over the Atlantic.

➤ **Banks**
Bank of Scotland, Harbour Street, Tarbert, tel. 01880 820848
Bank of Scotland, George Street, Oban, tel. 01631 563639

➤ **Launderettes**
  Oban Quality Launderette, Stevenson Street, Oban, tel. 01631 565866
  Oban Washtub, 5 Airds Place, Oban, tel. 01631 563265

➤ **Mountain Biking**
  Details on routes are available from the Forestry Commission at Lochgilphead,
  tel. 01546 602518, and Oban, tel. 01631 566155.

Tarbert has a lovely sheltered harbour popular with fishermen and
yachtsmen, and is enjoying a new lease of life now that a ferry across
Loch Fyne is operating. Tarbert Castle is worth a visit. It is a pleasant
ruin, if a bit unsafe, linked with Robert the Bruce, who extended it in
the 14thC. The present tower dates from the 1490s. Tarbert was
once a major centre for herring landings.

Further along the route is Lochgilphead, a bustling little town at the
start of the Crinan Canal, Britain's shortest. The canal has a lovely
towpath which is a beautiful and easy cycle. You can watch the
yachties trying to suss out how the locks work.

Continue north on the A816, following signs for Oban. The whole
area is packed with prehistoric remains, many of which are signposted, free and well worth exploring. At Dunadd Fort, kings of Dalriada
were crowned on the Stone of Destiny before it was taken to Scone,
then stolen by Edward I and taken to England in 1296. The stone
resided until November 1996 in Westminster Abbey, though it was
temporarily liberated by Scottish Nationalists in 1950 – a cause of
great public jubilation. The stone is now on display at Edinburgh
Castle on the basis that it will be taken to London to be used in
future coronation ceremonies. The site at Dunadd is a series of
defended terraces. The summit has a rock-carved boar and a carved
footprint in the rock. Further north are two stone circles dating from
3000 BC.

Kilmartin lies on the A816 and has a cemetery containing interesting
medieval carved gravestones. It also has a friendly pub. The whole
area round Kilmartin is wonderful, with rolling hills and views out to
the Paps of Jura. Two miles further north you pass Carnassarie Castle
on the left, built for John Carswell who translated some of John
Knox's doctrines into Gaelic. The resulting book, *The Book of
Common Order*, was the first to be printed in Gaelic in 1567. ➤ 36

A National Trust garden, Arduaine, planted in the early 1900s by James Arthur Campbell and designed by Osgood Mackenzie, is famous for its spring flowers. The Gulf Stream provides a unique micro-climate which encourages the plants, such as rhododendrons and azaleas, to grow to an unusually large size. There is a tearoom. (Admission charge.)

Further on at Kilninver it is worth a detour on the B844 to Clachan and Seil Island to see the elegant Bridge over the Atlantic, built in 1791. On the island side is one of the Highlands' most characterful pubs, the Tigh an Truish or 'House of the Trousers', which is where the islanders would change into trousers when the kilt was banned following the Jacobite risings. Seil Island itself is lovely, and this may be a good place to break your journey overnight. A ferry operates to tiny Easdale Island where there is a Folk Museum. (Admission charge.)

Head back to the A816 and pass the Culfail Hotel, at the head of Loch Melfort, which is ivy-covered and comfortable. Continue to Oban along the shores of Loch Feochan. Glenfeochan House Gardens, 3 miles beyond Kilninver, have many trees which were planted in the mid-19thC, plus a walled garden. (Admission charge.)

Oban is a bustling town, one of the best places on the West Coast both visually and for facilities. Look out for islanders seemingly baffled by the undoubtedly cosmopolitan ways of Obanites! It is overlooked by McCaig's Folly, a 19thC circular ruin reminiscent of the Colosseum and the brainchild of local banker John Stuart McCaig, partly to ease unemployment in the town. It can be reached on foot up Craigard Street and there are good views out to Mull, Kerrera and Lismore, and across to the Morvern Peninsula. Oban Distillery has regular tours (admission charge), while A World in Miniature (admission charge) has an unusual display of tiny rooms, models and dioramas. Oban Sealife Centre, tel. 01631 720386, is 10 miles north of Oban and has sharks, seals and rays. (Admission charge.) The town has a couple of Indian restaurants, but the un-Indian and unique Mactavish's Kitchen on George Street is where everyone tends to end up.

Route 8: Islay & Jura

See Fact Sheet 6

◆

Stage 1: Islay

It is a 2 hour crossing from Kennacraig to Islay, with two possible destinations. I arrived at Port Ellen in the south, but other services head for Port Askaig on the east coast, in the strait between Islay and Jura, where the tide hurtles through like a river. Arriving at Port Ellen by ferry, you pass several whisky distilleries, including Lagavulin and Laphroaig, before arriving in this quiet and well-kept little town, with white-painted houses and a sandy beach. Islay is flat with fertile agricultural land, but many of the island's 4000 inhabitants are employed at the various distilleries which make Islay malts famous across the world. The grain used is not grown on the island but Islay's distinctive peaty water is crucial to the taste of the whisky. Islay whisky provides employment for many of the island's inhabitants and is exported around the world. Tours of the distilleries at Lagavulin and Laphroaig are worth a detour on the little road east of Port Ellen. No trip to Islay would be complete without visiting at least one distillery. Further on is Kildalton Church, with one of the finest early-Christian crosses dating from the 9thC.

Islay has long been of strategic importance. It was a Viking settlement from 800 until 1156, and later was the headquarters of the Lords of the Isles, ancestors of Clan Donald, who controlled from their stronghold in Loch Finlaggan much of the western seaboard from the Mull of Kintyre to Cape Wrath until 1493. The title of Lord of the Isles still exists and is held by the Prince of Wales.

I took the little road just west of Port Ellen to Kintra, which has a great sandy beach, pony trekking and the Kintra Outdoor Centre. This is just north of the rugged Oa Peninsula, once inhabited by smugglers and the operators' illegal whisky stills. Kintra has a restaurant, a pub, and a bunkhouse which will take families. As a place for staying and lazing around with a group of friends or *en famille*, this is a good bet.

Bowmore is one of the prettier island villages. It was planned in the 18thC and has a well-kept whitewashed air. The distillery, tel. 01496 810254, is Islay's largest and has the best-organized tour, with audiovisual presentations. While you are are learning about mashing and malting, the children can splash about in the nearby swimming pool, heated by waste heat from the distillery.

➤ 40

Islay & Jura

Fact Sheet 6 . . . .

Both these beautiful islands are suitable for relaxed, quiet cycling. Islay is flat and agricultural, and is famous for its whisky. There are a number of tourist facilities. The island's marvellous festival features folk bands, whisky tasting and much more. Jura, by contrast, is magnificently barren and rocky.

➤ **OS Maps 60, 61**

➤ **Tourist Information Office**
Bowmore (see Fact Sheet on pages 26-7)

➤ **Ferries**
Lochranza, Arran-Claonaig (April-October)/Kennacraig, Kintyre-Port Ellen, Islay-Port Askaig, Islay-Colonsay-Oban (Wednesday only, April-October) Caledonian Macbrayne, tel. 01475 650100
Feolin Ferry, Jura-Port Askaig, Islay. Very regular service. Western Ferries, tel. 01496 840681

➤ **Cycle Shops**
MacAulay & Torrie, Port Ellen, Islay, tel. 01496 302053. Bike hire.
Brian Palmer, 44 Stanalane, Bowmore, Islay, tel. 01496 810653. Repairs.
Robert Murphy, Bruichladdich, tel. 01496 850397. Bike hire.
Bike hire is also available at the Post Office, Bowmore.
On Jura there are no bike facilities, so don't break down!

➤ **Hostels**
Accommodation on Islay and particularly Jura is very limited, so book in advance via the Tourist Information Office in Bowmore.
SYHA, Port Charlotte, Islay, tel. 01496 850385
Kintra Outdoor Centre, Kintra, near Port Ellen, tel. 01496 302051. Hostel, tea-room and a great beach.
On Jura try the following (all in Craighouse):
Mrs Mach, tel. 01496 820217/820230/820304
Mrs Boardman, tel. 01496 820379
Mrs Miller, tel. 01496 820311

➤ **Banks**
Bank of Scotland, Shore Street, Bowmore, tel. 01496 810437
Royal Bank of Scotland, Main Street, Bowmore, tel. 01496 810555

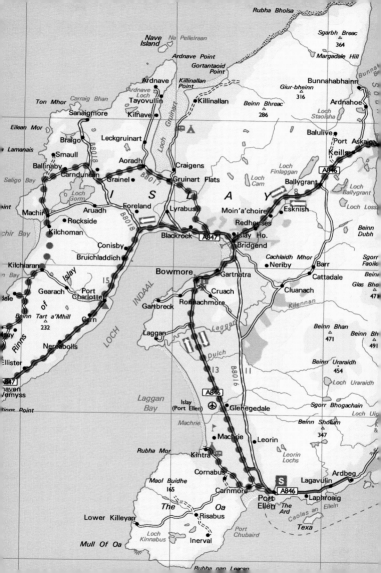

From Bowmore it is a gentle cycle to Bridgend, where there is a shop selling ice cream, food and much else, and the Bridgend Hotel, which stands at the crossroads of the island. A bench outside affords a good view of the island going about its business, from little tractors to the laird's car sweeping into Islay House. Bridgend has some pleasant leafy trees, which are something of a rarity round here.

The Rhinns of Islay stretch west past Bruichladdich (another malt), giving pleasant views across the bay. Port Charlotte has a particularly nice youth hostel, which is fairly new. It shares a building with the Islay Field Centre, which has information on local fauna and flora. Port Charlotte also has the Museum of Islay Life and a creamery. The museum contains an illicit still. (Admission charge.) At the southern tip of the Rhinns is the incongruous time warp village of Portnahaven, once a busy fishing port. Now it is busy with tourists, as it is undoubtedly very pretty.

From Portnahaven I followed the west coast. I stopped at Tormisdale and visited a signposted craft shop where lovely fabrics and hand-knitted jumpers were displayed. Further north at Kilchiaran Farm, branch off the road and pass a rock draped with lichen called the Granny's or Lady's Rock. Machir Bay is named after the classic flower mat that covers the shore in early summer. There is a delightful path covered in primroses, yellow violets and daisies above the pristine sandy beach. Navigating is not hard but OS map 60 is helpful. However, if you keep the Atlantic to your left you should be OK. When you hit the road at the north end of Machir Bay, head west back to Bridgend on the B8017 north of Loch Gorm. There are no tea stops on this part of the route so bring a picnic. Just north is Gruinart Nature Reserve, complete with a RSPB visitor centre, which is a haven in winter for barnacle geese from Greenland. Islay has a goose officer employed by Scottish Natural Heritage to see to the wellbeing of these birds.

Stage 2: Port Askaig & Jura

At Bridgend branch off to Port Askaig and Jura. It is only 8 miles to Port Askaig and the ferry to Jura, but with a headwind it is completely wild. On a good day you could do this stretch in an hour as it is quite flat and on fine roads, but the day I did it, it took over 3 hours, with a few rest stops. For the first bit I cheated because I tucked myself in behind a tiny and ancient tractor which was rolling along at

an easy pace and used its slipstream to help me along. I stopped again at the Ballygrant Inn, where they were just lighting the fires and the rooms filled up with smoke, blown down the chimney, till we started choking. Still, it was very cosy when the peat was alight.

At Port Askaig the ferry whisks you across the channel where the current flows at up to 8 knots, and you get great views of the Paps (breasts) of Jura. If you are going to climb these mountains be prepared, for there are three of them. It must be said that there is not massive scope for cycling on Jura because there is only one road. But the island is well worth visiting for its incredible wildness and remoteness, and the folk living there are very friendly. The road runs along the east side of the island for 25 miles to Lagg, before gradually deteriorating into a very rough track at the north of the island, where people go to see the spectacular Corryvreckan Whirlpool, comparable to the Maelstrom in ferocity.

If you get this far you will pass George Orwell's house by Ardlussa, used by the author while writing Nineteen Eighty-Four. But the bleak moor and whistling wind weakened me, and when I arrived at Jura House, a fertile oasis set among big trees, I stopped. There is a garden open to the public – put your money in an honesty box – and walk through bluebell woods down to the shore. On your return, enter the house grounds, squeezing through tool sheds, and emerge in a walled garden full of flowers and vegetables.

The main settlement on Jura is Craighouse, and it is here that you will find the Jura Distillery. Book an appointment on 01496 820332.

Finding accommodation was a bit of a panic on this sleepy island. Despite being remote and apparently quiet, all the B&Bs fill up quickly and it was very late as I headed towards the caravan I had finally negotiated. The sun setting behind the Paps was startlingly beautiful, and deer with their antlers in velvet started away from the road, an appropriate image as Jura means 'Deer Island' in Gaelic.

◆ Route 9: Cowal Peninsula

◆ ### See Fact Sheet 7

The ferry from Tarbert on Kintyre arrives at Portavadie. This used to be a pretty village before a misguided government initiative built the harbour and reputedly the biggest hole in Scotland. The idea was to build oil rigs but the demand never materialized. In spite, or perhaps because of this, the Cowal Peninsula is still a lovely quiet haven, with beautiful forests and light traffic, which is remarkable as it is so close to Glasgow.

Fact Sheet 7 .... # Cowal Peninsula & Bute

The new ferry from Tarbert in Kintyre to Portavadie on the Cowal Peninsula is ideal for tourists. The seascapes and mountains of the Cowal Peninsula are spectacular, though Dunoon has seen better days. The US base at Holy Loch is now deserted and the area is having to adapt to its new circumstances. Rothesay was once a major resort for Glaswegian holidaymakers and still has a number of attractions.

➤ **OS Maps 55, 56, 62, 63**

➤ **Tourist Information Offices**
   Dunoon and Rothesay (see Fact Sheet on pages 26-7)

➤ **Ferries**
   Colintraive, Cowal-Rhubodach, Bute, Tarbert-Portavadie, Gourock-Dunoon, Wemyss Bay-Rothesay
   Caledonian Macbrayne, tel. 01475 650100
   Dunoon-Gourock
   Western Ferries, tel. 01369 704452

➤ **Cycle Shops**
   Calder Bros, 7 Bridge Street, Rothesay, tel. 01700 504477
   Highland Stores, 152 Argyll Street, Dunoon, tel. 01369 702001
   Montgomery & Sons, Strachur Filling Station, tel. 01369 860227

➤ **Hostels**
   SYHA, Tighnabruaich, tel. 01700 811622. Near Portavadie.

➤ **Banks**
   Bank of Scotland, 78 Argyll Street, Dunoon, tel. 01369 702045
   Bank of Scotland, 36 Montague Street, Rothesay, tel. 01369 703851

➤ **Mountain Biking**
   For details of forest trails, contact the Forestry Commission, Kilmun, Dunoon, tel. 01369 840666.

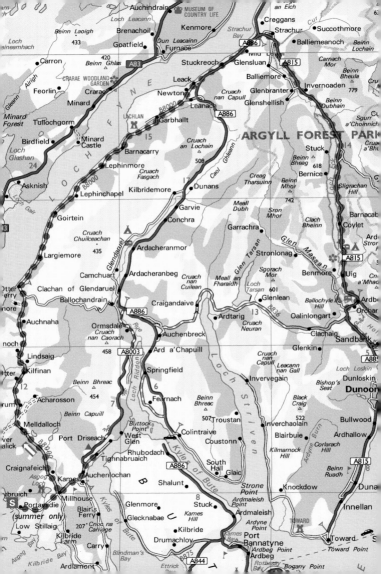

The route follows a small road with some hill climbs and places where the road follows the loch. At Tighnabruaich, on the B8000, there is a youth hostel and various restaurants. At the north of the route is Strachur and the famous Creggans Inn, tel. 01369 860279, which serves both gourmet and bar food. It was owned by the veteran explorer and Tory MP, the late Sir Fitzroy Maclean, who is thought to have been a role model for local author Ian Fleming's character James Bond. On the way to Strachur is Otter Ferry, with the Oystercatcher Restaurant, tel. 01700 821229. The name is thought to originate from *oiter*, which in Gaelic means 'sandbank'. At low tide a sandbank stretching a mile out into Loch Fyne is visible.

Turn southeast through Glenbranter on the A815. The Forestry Commission has various waymarked off-road cycle routes in the area. About 10 miles south is Loch Coylet with the Whistlefield Hotel, and then the Coylet Inn, tel. 01369 840322, a drovers' inn with great open fires, friendly locals and simple accommodation.

Further on towards Dunoon are signs for the Younger Botanic Garden, which is highly recommended in May and June. It is part of the network of gardens run by the Royal Botanic Gardens in Edinburgh and has Britain's finest Wellingtonia, as well as rhododendrons and magnolia collections. Tearoom. (Admission charge.)

Dunoon is a ferry port and until recently was where the US Navy had a base, which gave local businesses a leg-up. However, as part of the peace dividend this base has been closed and the Americans have gone home, leaving the town a bit sad. There are still some elderly taxis painted with Stars and Stripes and a couple of burger bars but the US influence has largely disappeared, except on the bottom of Holy Loch where junk, including the odd missile, is piled high. Local scrap merchants are rumoured to have expressed interest in getting the missiles up for their metal, much to the consternation of the local council! Dunoon Castle has a rich history, even though there isn't much to see nowadays. Owned by Robert the Bruce and Edward Balliol, it was taken by the Stewarts in 1371 then passed to the Earls of Argyll on condition that they supply a red rose on demand. The Burns Statue nearby is of Highland Mary, one of the Bard's many lovers.

Route 10: Rothesay & the Kyles of Bute

See Fact Sheet 7

Rothesay is the main town on Bute and is a fascinating place, built by the Glasgow middle classes as a summer watering hole. The Winter Gardens are a reminder of times past, and so too are the magnificent award-winning Victorian public toilets – an essential place of pilgrimage. There are even conducted tours, tel. 01700 504754 for details. Rothesay Castle (admission charge) is a more conventional and equally fine tourist attraction. It was restored by the Marquises of Bute, whose home is now Mount Stuart House, a great Victorian confection designed and built in 1879 by Robert Rowand Anderson. The house has now been opened to the public during the summer by the father and mother-in-law of racing driver Johnny Dumfries, the present marquis. Tearoom. (Admission charge.)

The southwest of Bute has interesting cycling, as the road follows the contours of rolling hills and passes sandy bays. Ettrick Bay has standing stones and a nearby tearoom.

Don't miss the island's festivals. The Bute Jazz festival is in early May and the Folk Festival in July. And, yes folks, the Country and Westerners have their hoedowns and shoot-outs in September.

It is entirely feasible and satisfying to do a tour of Bute, about 25 miles, in a day and take the ferry back to Wemyss Bay. However, the route suggested here takes you across to the Cowal Peninsula on the little ferry from Rhubodach to Colintraive and then heads east on the B836, which is quite hilly. This magnificent bleak road passes the wonderfully named Loch Tarsan. There are good views but no tearooms until Dunoon, so take a picnic. From Dunoon (see Route 9) take the ferry back to Gourock, just up the Clyde coast from Wemyss Bay. This is quite an adventurous and satisfying route for a weekend as it feels so remote.

Route 11: Round Great Cumbrae

See Fact Sheet 8 and Map for Route 10

Great Cumbrae is a friendly little island which is ideal for family cycling. A good road goes round the whole of the island and there is also the option of a steady climb and exciting descent back down into Millport across the centre of the island. There is the adventure of the ferry crossing and a cycling distance which is a challenge for kids but is easily do-able. It is a 10-year-old's paradise, with sandy bays, safe beaches and pleasant little roads. Bute has some rolling farmland, and an aquarium at the Marine Station managed by the University of London, though it is presently under threat from funding changes affecting UK universities. Millport also has the smallest cathedral in Britain, which is still in use. The town is the island's main centre, and is popular with Glaswegians in summer.

Fact Sheet 8 . . . . **Cumbrae**

Cumbrae is a favourite place to go 'Doon the Watter' (the Clyde) from Glasgow. One of the main pastimes is to hire bikes and cycle right round the island, a distance of about 8 miles.

➤ **OS Map 63**

➤ **Rail**
A regular train service operates from Glasgow Central to Largs.

➤ **Ferries**
There is a regular ferry service between approximately 7 am and 7 pm for the 10 min trip from Largs to Cumbrae Slip.
Caledonian Macbrayne, tel. 01475 650100

➤ **Cycle Shops**
Bremmers, Millport, tel. 01475 530309/530707. Bike hire.
Mapes of Millport, Guildford Street, Millport, tel. 01475 530444. Bike hire.

THE WESTERN ISLES

The Western Isles are the most varied and wonderful group of islands, and provide a unique cycling experience. The mixture of huge sandy beaches, wild flower meadows and Neolithic remains make the islands incredibly interesting, and the roads are very quiet. The islands, however, are deceptively big and at times when it is windy, cycling can be quite arduous. The predominant wind direction is from the southwest. However, they are normally suitable for adventurous people, including families. The southern islands tend to be Catholic and less strict than the Presbyterian north, where the Sabbath is very firmly kept. It is frowned on to arrive or leave on a Sunday, so treat it as a day of rest. If your soul doesn't appreciate it, your knees will.

The best cycling route is from the south, taking the ferry from Oban, or possibly flying to Barra, where the plane lands on the beach. Unofficially there is often room on the plane for a bike. By starting in the south, the chances are that this route north will be downwind.

If you catch the ferry to Ullapool you are about 60 miles from Inverness, the nearest main railhead. The road near Inverness involves some busy dual carriageway and is not very bicycle-friendly. However, if you are carrying on, the mainland north of Ullapool is magnificent cycling country (see Chapter 6). Alternatively, coaches connect Ullapool to Inverness. These meet the ferry and take bikes subject to availability. For details, contact Highland Omnibus, tel. 01463 718282. From Inverness trains south have very limited space for bikes, and booking is essential. Logistically it may be easier to go by car to Uig on Skye and then take Route 13. This is also useful if you don't want to take long ferry journeys.

➤ **Route 12 (Grand Tour)**
Ludag/Lochboisdale-Stornoway
♦ Long but easy, unless cycling into the wind. 192/185 miles.

➤ **Route 13**
North Uist & South Harris
♦ Mainly easy, but some steep hills on East Harris. 75 miles.

➤ **Route 14**
Barra, Vatersay & Eriskay
♦ Easy. 22 miles.

➤ **Rail**
Oban is the nearest railhead for the Western Isles, with 3-4 trains daily from Glasgow Queen Street. The trains often connect with the ferries. Tel. 0345 484950 (enquiries) or 0345 550033 (bookings).

➤ **Ferries**

Lochmaddy, North Uist-Uig, Skye/Oban-Lochboisdale, South Uist and Castlebay, Barra/Lochboisdale-Castlebay/Newton Ferry-Berneray-Leverburgh Caledonian Macbrayne, tel. 01475 650100
Eoligarry, Barra-Ludag, South Uist
Private ferry, tel. 01878 720233. 4 ferries daily. May be replaced by a Caledonian Macbrayne ferry in future.

➤ **Airlines**

This area is so remote it may be worth considering flying if you have limited time. Bikes are allowed, space permitting. For details, contact British Airways, tel. 0345 222111. There are flights from Glasgow or Inverness to Stornoway, Barra or Benbecula.

➤ **Cycle Tour Organizers**

Bespoke and SYHA Island-hopping. See page 227

➤ **Tourist Information Offices (Open all year)**

Stornoway, Lewis, 4 South Beach Street, tel. 01851 703088

➤ **Special Events**

Barra Feis, held in early July, is a fantastic folk festival.

GRAND TOUR

Route 12: Ludag/Lochboisdale-Stornoway

See Fact Sheets 9 and 10

Stage 1: South Uist

The route starts at Lochboisdale on South Uist. However, some cyclists will come from Barra and Eriskay (see Route 14). If you do this, you will land at Ludag. A couple of miles on is the Pollachar Inn, tel. 01878 700215, which has a spectacular location and is much frequented by the locals. This used to be a delightful old-fashioned pub, but it has recently been modernized. Head to Dalabrog and then take the A865 into Lochboisdale, the main ferry port and settlement on South Uist.

North from Lochboisdale is the small South Uist Museum (free), 5 miles beyond Dalabrog. There is also the statue to Our Lady of the

Isles, which was put up by the locals in 1957 to protect them from the missiles being tested by the military close to the island of St Kilda. A worthwhile detour just past this is to take the turn marked to Bornais and out to Rubha Ardvule, a spectacular sandy spit of land with a lochan and an ancient fort.

The sandy beaches on South Uist are magnificent and some hardy people cycle along them, although I doubt if it does the bikes much good. North on the main road is the cottage where Flora Macdonald was born. You may wish to pick your way up the little farm roads past Staoinebrig and round the coast to Snishival. From here it is not far to Howmore (Tobha Mor), where there is a Gatcliff Trust Hostel in a traditional black house, and bike facilities, tel. 01878 700237, run by Tommy Macdonald, who is enthusiastic and happy to share his cycling knowledge.

➤ 54

Fact Sheet 9 · · · · · · · · · · · · · · **The Uists & Barra**

➤ **OS Maps 18, 22, 31**

➤ **Tourist Information Offices (Summer only)**
Lochmaddy, North Uist, Pier Road, tel. 018763 321
Lochboisdale, South Uist, Pier Road, tel. 018784 286
Castlebay, Barra, Main Street, tel. 018714 336

➤ **Cycle Shops**
Alex Dan Cycle Centre, Kenneth Street, Stornoway, tel. 01851 704025. Spares and repairs.
Tommy Macdonald, 9 Howmore, South Uist, tel. 01870 620283/610231 (work). Bike repairs. Close to Howmore hostel.
John McDougall, Castlebay, Barra, tel. 01871 810284. Bike hire.
Margaret Macdonald, Lochside Cottage, 27 Lochboisdale, tel. 01878 700472. Bike hire, and cyclist-friendly food and accommodation.

➤ **Hostels**
SYHA, Lochmaddy, North Uist, Pier Road, tel. 01876 500368
Gatcliff Trust, Howmore, South Uist. Sleeping bag required.

➤ **Banks**
Bank of Scotland, Lochmaddy, tel. 01876 500323
Bank of Scotland, Balivanich, Benbecula, tel. 01870 602044. Cashpoint.
Royal Bank of Scotland, Dalabrog, South Uist, tel. 01878 700399
Royal Bank of Scotland, Castlebay, Barra, tel. 01871 810291
Other areas are covered by the rural travelling bank. Ask the locals for details.

Howmore also has some important historic chapels and headstones, almost as important and far less hyped than those on Iona. The Loch Druidibeg Nature Reserve just north of Howmore has greylag geese and corncrakes. About 6 miles from Howmore is a shop at Clachan and down the road to the right is the Orasay Inn, which serves food and coffee.

Stage 2: Benbecula & North Uist

Cross from South Uist to Benbecula on many causeways. This is a good place to see birds and wildlife, including seals and the occasional otter. Benbecula is dominated by the RAF base and is quite busy by Hebridean standards. A community centre at Lionacleit has a tearoom, as has the airport. Opposite the airport a small shop, Macgilveray's, has good-value Harris jumpers and other local goods. The Dark Isles Hotel at Lionacleit is OK, and there is a bank at Balivanich.

Another series of causeways leads to North Uist. About a mile after Corunna is a turnoff to the Cladach Baleshare. At one time this was a hostel, but at the time of writing it is closed. It may reopen, so check with the Tourist Information Office. At Clachan there's a good food shop, but not much else. The direct road from Clachan to Lochmaddy is not particularly interesting, but the Langais Hotel is good for a coffee stop and there is a very fine chambered cairn and standing stones about 2 miles along.

The best tourist route is to carry on round the west coast of the island on the A865. The Westford Inn, tel. 01876 580653, about 4 miles north of Clachan, is a strange wooden building, but it allows camping and has the best pub food on the islands.

Further round, the Balranald Nature Reserve is crammed with breeding birds, and there is open access to the RSPB display. The white sandy beaches and wild flowers around here are superb. Lochmaddy is on the east side of North Uist and has a hostel, food shops and ferry terminal. It also has the Lochmaddy Hotel, tel. 01876 500331, which is OK. However, the best thing to do in these parts is to take the little ferry at the end of the B893, north of Lochmaddy, from Newton Ferry to Berneray (Prince Charles' favourite island), which has a superb Gatcliff Trust hostel with peat fires and a thatched roof. There is also a shop and a café, and otters play in the bay.

Fact Sheet 10 . . . .

Harris & Lewis

➤ OS Maps 8, 13, 18

➤ Tourist Information Offices (Summer only)
  Tarbert, Harris, Pier Road, tel. 01859 502011

➤ Cycle Shops
  D.M. Mackenzie, Pier Road, Tarbert, tel. 01859 502271. Bike hire.
  Alex Dan Cycle Centre, Kenneth Street, Stornoway, tel. 01851 704025. Repairs
  and spares.

➤ Hostels
  SYHA, Stockinish, East Harris, tel. 01859 530373
  Stornoway Independent Hostel, 47 Keith Street, tel. 01851 703628
  Gatcliff Trust hostels are inexpensive, laid-back hostels, where sleeping bags
  are needed. No telephones and no advance booking.
  Rhenigidale (Reinigeadal), on south side of Loch Seaforth.
  Garenin (Gearrannan) Youth Hostel, Carloway, near Calanais, Lewis. A restored
  thatched black house.
  Berneray Gatcliff Trust Hostel. Sleeping bag and own food required.
  Thatched roof.

➤ Banks
  Royal Bank of Scotland, 17 North Beach, Stornoway, Lewis, tel. 01851 705252
  Bank of Scotland, 45 Cromwell Street, Stornoway, Lewis, tel. 01851 704000
  Bank of Scotland, Tarbert, Harris, tel. 01859 502453
  Other areas are covered by the rural travelling bank. Ask the locals for details.

➤ Launderette
  Erica's, Macaulay Road, Stornoway, Lewis, tel. 01851 704508

Stage 3: Harris

From Berneray, the recommended route is to land at Leverburgh,
and explore one of the most beautiful islands anywhere. The west
coast of Harris has mind-blowing sandy beaches and turquoise water.
The east coast road – the so-called Golden Road, because of what it
cost to build – runs through magnificent rocky scenery which resem-
bles a lunar landscape. There are little croft houses where you can go
and look at Harris tweed still being handmade on noisy old looms.
However, there is a move to introduce more modern looms, but they
are only gaining ground slowly.

The recommended route is via the west coast because the beaches are unmissable. It is worth taking the cut-off to Luskentyre. There's B&B heaven with Mrs Morrison at Seaview, Croft 10, tel. 01859 550263. The east coast is beautiful but hilly. Staying at the youth hostel at Stockinish, you may well see otters frolicking in the sea. Drinshader Independent Hostel, tel. 01851 511255, about 5 miles southeast of Tarbert, is well situated.

Tarbert is a pleasant little Highland town with a ferry to Skye or Lochmaddy, plus shops, a bank, a barber, bike hire and the marvellous Rose Villa Tearoom. If you notice something weird about the Harris Hotel, which makes a good coffee stop, it is that it has trees outside! If you are hostelling, the Rhenigidale (Reinigeadal) Gatcliff Trust hostel is down a side road 8 miles north of Tarbert, on Loch Seaforth in a restored croft.

Stage 4: Lewis

The first part – about 40 miles – of this route is quite dull. There is also nothing by way of tea stops, so take food with you. Several B&Bs are available around Baile Ailein near Loch Erisort. Continue on the A859 for about 7 miles. Turn left on a minor road to Acha Mor and continue to Gearraidh na h'Aibhne, which has shops and cafés.

Callanish Standing Stones are well signposted and 2 miles north of the village. These are the best-known of a number of Bronze-Age remains that exist in this part of Lewis. Dating from 2000 BC, these stones and the other 20 sites suggest this area was once a major centre. There are 13 standing stones rising up to 20 ft high. The stones are arranged like a cross and there are theories that they may have been for astronomical use. Most of the stones are made of Lewisian gneiss and each has a strange sculptural quality – almost a personality of its own. The recently-built visitor centre has proved controversial but provides useful information. (Admission charge.)

Further on is Carloway Broch, spectacularly well preserved. Accommodation is available at Gearrannan, another of the Gatcliff Trust hostels, and again a black house. Further up there is a black house at Arnol with peat fires burning. From here the recommended route loops back on the A857.

A worthwhile diversion is to head out west from Gearraidh na h'Aibhne to Timsgearraidh, where there is a nice medium-priced

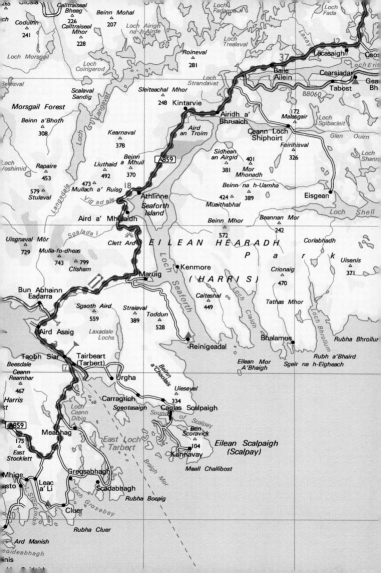

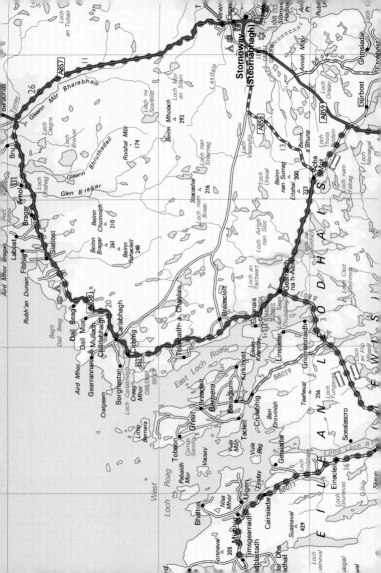

country hotel, Baile na Cille, tel. 01851 672242, which welcomes children and serves sandwiches for lunch. It has a few lower price rooms and some bikes for hire.

Stornoway is the capital of the Western Isles, with all services. For a cultural visit, there's the Museum Nan Eilean (free) in Francis Street or the An Lanntair Art Gallery (free) in the town hall. Ali's Tandoori Restaurant, 24 South Beach Street, tel. 01851 706116, is open on the Sabbath.

Route 13: North Uist & South Harris
See Fact Sheets 9 and 10, and third Map for Route 12

This route partly covers the territory of the Grand Tour, so read Route 12 as well to get a full picture. It will give you the opportunity to explore North Uist, Berneray and Harris in more depth than the Grand Tour allows.

The route starts where the ferry arrives at Lochmaddy, on the east coast of North Uist, and heads southwest to Clachan. Instead of heading down to Benbecula, which you could do, the route then heads up the delightful west coast of North Uist. The huge beaches and machair (wild flower meadow fertilized by shells) is beautiful. Inland, a couple of roads climb onto moorland where birds of prey, including eagles, falcons and various owls, are commonly seen hunting. The Balranald Nature Reserve is also well worth visiting and is rich in sea birds. Beware of hostile arctic terns pecking at you. The Westford Inn, tel. 01876 580653, is the place to eat and is about 4 miles from Clachan.

The north end of North Uist is a pleasant mix of sandy bays and crofting townships where the appealing smell of peat smoke drifts from the chimneys. The route turns off the A865 onto the B893 signposted to Newton Ferry and Ludag, from where the ferry leaves. If possible, take the ferry and stay overnight on the delightful island of Berneray at the Gatcliff Trust hostel. Bear in mind that facilities on the island are basic, so bring essentials, including a sleeping bag. Alternatively, try B&Bs via the Tourist Information Offices on the other Western Isles.

Continue north on the ferry to Harris and land at Leverburgh. Head up to the main Tarbert road for 0.5 mile, then turn right to Roghadal where you can visit the 12thC St Clement's Church. The Rodel Hotel was once visited by Queen Elizabeth, but has now declined seriously. The mountain behind the village, Roneval, has been targetted as a 'superquarry' and an English firm is seeking to turn it into a pile of aggregate. Local opinion on the issue is mixed. Some want it as a source of employment, while others wish to retain the beauty of the place. Visitors generally are shocked at the prospect of this wild land being subject to major industrial development. At the time of writing the result of a Public Enquiry is awaited.

The landscape on the east coast of Harris is quite extraordinarily wild and rugged, with a peculiar beauty. Land raids occurred here after World War I, when angry crofters seized their land. It is a harsh and inhospitable landscape. In this area many crofters supplement their income by making Harris tweed (see feature on page 63) and many of the looms can be heard clattering noisily. Excellent woolly jumpers can be bought here much cheaper than in shops elsewhere. However, there is nothing much along here in the way of tearooms, so be prepared.

After Aird Mhige, at the head of Loch Stockinish, turn right (southeast) to continue the coastal route. A mile along is the Stockinish Youth Hostel, and a fine place it is. The wildlife in the bay is extraordinary, and otters are seen regularly. If you continue round the coast, turn right again at the end of Loch Grosebay. This road is known as the Golden Road locally because it cost so much to build. At Drimminsadder is an independent hostel, and a craft shop demonstrating tweed-weaving. When you emerge onto the main A859 you could head north into Tarbert, from where ferries take you back to Uig on Skye. Alternatively, the route returns to Leverburgh along the west coast of Harris, which enjoys Caribbean-turquoise water and stunning sands. It is certainly worth a detour west of 5 miles to Losgaintir to enjoy the amazing beaches. If you complete the trip you will pass the Macleod and the Scarista standing stones, both of which have very atmospheric situations. This section again is devoid of coffee stops, though a café does operate at the Coop at Clachan south of Sgarasta Mhor. From Leverburgh you could return to North Uist and Lochmaddy, and complete the figure of eight. Alternatively, retrace your steps to Tarbert.

HARRIS TWEED

Harris tweed is a woven wool cloth authenticated by the orb trade-mark of the Harris Tweed Association. Tweed was first introduced in the 1840s by Lady Dunsmore to relieve the disastrous famines and remains a vital part of the island's economy today. The weaving of the cloth fits in well with the crofting lifestyle, as it can be done part time between agricultural pursuits. The tweed cloth is woven on hand-powered looms in the croft houses of Harris and Lewis. If you pause in many of the island villages you will hear the loud clatter of the old Hattersley looms which have been used for decades. Many of these weaving sheds have signs outside inviting visitors. Recently the Bonas Griffiths hand loom has begun to be introduced; it is faster than the Hattersley but doesn't have the same character. Traditionally the wool is dyed different colours with plants such as lichens.

Route 14: Barra, Vatersay & Eriskay

See Fact Sheet 9 and first Map for Route 12

Castlebay is a pretty if sprawling crofting township and is the main settlement on Barra. It has a bank and a post office, and a nice tea-room close to both. Mr McDougal hires out bikes, tel. 01871 810284. The public bar of the Isle of Barra Hotel, tel. 01871 810223, is the hub of the island. The island has a road round it which forms a 12 mile loop. It is well worth a detour over to Vatersay, a small sister island which is enjoying a new lease of life after a causeway linked it to Barra in 1991. This causeway is beyond Nask and was built after a prize bull drowned while swimming to Barra. Another alleged reason was that local men found it hard to persuade women from Barra to move to the island. Vatersay has some beautiful sandy beaches.

The west coast of Barra is studded with little bays and sandy beaches. The modern Western Isles Hotel at Tangusdale, tel. 01871 810383, 2 miles from Castlebay, is good for a lunch stop. The other place to have tea and buns is the remarkable little airport shed at Traigh Mor at the north end of the island. This serves sporadically when the plane is due (at low tide). The scheduled air service is unique in Western Europe and the locals are proud of their runway which gets washed twice a day. However, the islanders have recently voted in a referendum to go for a 'proper' runway, but the site is still a source of debate. It therefore appears likely that the current situation will continue for some time yet. The beach is also used by local crofters who have raked cockles for centuries as a food source.

Some B&Bs serve evening meals in Eolaigearraidh (Eoligarry), if you book in advance. If possible, get the little ferry from Eolaigearraidh to Eriskay, where the SS *Politician* went aground during World War II. This incident gave rise to the famous *Whisky Galore!*, written by Compton Mackenzie, which was made into a delightful Ealing comedy. The Politician Pub, which is actually quite new and not as characterful as you might expect, is being converted into low-cost bunkhouse accommodation at the time of writing. Tel. 01878 720246 for up-to-date details. Ferry times vary but there are four services daily, tel. 01878 720233. However, Caledonian Macbrayne may well take over this route and put on a larger ferry.

Eriskay is also where Bonnie Prince Charlie first landed in Scotland. Other claims to fame are the Eriskay ponies and a unique plant, the sea bindweed, Latin name *Calystegia soldanella*. Generally, Eriskay is not ideal for cycling but it is a delightful place for exploring on foot.

MULL, SKYE, ORKNEY & SHETLAND

These islands are all different in character and are wonderful for exploration by bicycle. Mull is quiet and for the purist. Skye attracts hordes of visitors. Orkney and Shetland, despite being in the same area to the north of the Scottish mainland, are markedly different. Orkney has fertile farming land, whereas Shetland has a peaty, bleak landscape. Both islands are proud of their Scandinavian links. All island groups in this chapter are disjointed, so all appropriate information is in the detailed fact sheets.

➤ **Route 15**
Mull and Iona
♦♦ Moderate, with some steep hills. 106 miles.

➤ **Route 16**
Skye
♦♦ Moderate, with some hills. 141 miles.

➤ **Route 17**
Glenelg, southern Skye & Plockton
♦♦ Moderate, with one steep climb over to Glenelg. 60 miles.

➤ **Route18**
Orkney
♦ Generally easy, but very dependent on wind direction.

➤ **Route 19**
Shetland
♦ (♦) Easy to moderate, but very dependent on wind direction.

➤ **Rail & Ferries**
See details in the appropriate island fact sheet.

➤ **Cycle Tour Organizers**
Bespoke operates tours on Mull and Skye. See page 227.

➤ **Tourist Information Offices (Open all year)**
Tobermory, The Pier, Mull, tel. 01688 302182
Portree, Meall House, Skye, tel. 01478 612137
Kirkwall, 6 Broad Street, Orkney, tel. 01856 872856
Lerwick, Market Cross, Shetland, tel. 01599 693434

➤ **Special Events**
The year begins with Up Helly Aa, a traditional Viking festival, in Lerwick, Shetland. The St. Magnus Festival takes place in Orkney in June, followed by the Highland Games on Mull and the Skye Folk Festival in July.

Route 15: Mull & Iona

◆ **See Fact Sheet 11**

Stage 1: Craignure-Iona

Craignure is the main entry point to Mull. The ferry crossing from Oban is very pleasant, and passes Duart Castle, the 700-year-old stronghold of Clan Maclean, on its craggy promontory. Before leaving Craignure you may want to explore Torosay Castle – there is even a little steam train which goes there. The castle was designed by David Bryce in 1858 and is still cared for by its family owners. The furniture and artefacts are Victorian and include displays on wartime escapades and hunts for Nessie. The grounds have a formal garden with outstanding Italianate statues, as well as woodland and water gardens. (Admission charge.) Next door is Isle of Mull Weavers, where you can watch traditional weaving. Duart Castle is also open to the public and you can visit a dungeon where Spanish sailors from the wrecked and defeated Armada were held captive. The castle was for over 200 years part of the domain of the Lords of the Isles, who had their base at Finlaggan on Islay. (Admission charge.)

From the ferry pier turn left towards Fionnphort. The route over Glen More is a long climb, but the rewards are the wild scenery with great views over the Firth of Lorne, and back up Loch Linnhe towards Ben Nevis. The freewheel down to Kinloch Hotel is exhilarating and terrifying. Continue west towards Iona. The leg of land stretching west is known as the Ross of Mull, and there is quite good cycling alongside Loch Scridain. In Bunessan the Isle of Mull Wine Company does free tours and tastings of its Mull Riveter.

Fionnphort is the point from where thousands of tourists cross to Iona. The general store is very well stocked and there is also a restaurant, The Keel Row Bar.

Iona is an unusually beautiful island, only 3 miles long by 2 miles wide. St Columba arrived here from Ireland in AD 563, and founded a monastery from which Christianity spread. One of his monks, Aidan, is credited with establishing the community at Lindisfarne in Northumberland. Over 200,000 people visit Iona annually and it can feel swamped at times. The monastery has been restored and in front of it stand two magnificent Celtic crosses. ➢ 70

Fact Sheet 11

Mull

Mull is a favourite island – small, well formed and fairly accessible. The little roads in the west with views out over the Atlantic to Staffa, Coll and Tiree are breathtaking, but so are the hill climbs. Tobermory in the north is also one of the prettiest towns in the Hebrides, with its brightly painted buildings round the harbour. It is also well provided with tourist services.

➤ **OS Maps 47, 48, 49**

➤ **Tourist Information Office (Summer only)**
Craignure, The Pier, tel. 01680 812377

➤ **Ferries**
Oban-Craignure/Fishnish-Lochaline/Tobermory-Kilchoan.
Oban-Coll and Tiree calls at Tobermory 3 days a week.
Caledonian Macbrayne, tel. 01475 650100
Ulva Ferry. Ring the bell for ferry (no cars). Tel. 01688 500264. Tearoom.
Day trips from Ulva Ferry to Treshnish Isles and Staffa. Turus Mara, tel. 01688 400242
Day-long Sea Safaris from Tobermory, tel. 01688 302440

➤ **Rail**
Oban is the railhead for Mull and Iona.

➤ **Buses**
These carry bikes at the discretion of the driver. For further details contact Bowman's Coaches, Craignure, tel. 01680 812313.

➤ **Cycle Shops**
On Yer Bike (aka Fergus Whyte), Craignure, tel. 01680 812487, or Salen, tel. 01680 300501. The main place for bike hire, spares and repairs.
Pedal Power, Tobermory, tel. 01688 302007. Bike hire only.

➤ **Hostels**
SYHA, Tobermory, Main Street, tel. 01688 302481

➤ **Banks**
Clydesdale Bank, Main Street, Tobermory, tel. 0345 826818. Cashpoint.
The island is also served by a mobile bank.

➤ **Launderette**
Tobermory Launderette, 12 Main Street, tel. 01688 302132

Leaflets are available which describe the building and services are held daily in summer. Nearby, the chapel of St Oran may date from the 11thC and stands in the Reilig Oran, Britain's oldest cemetery and the burial place of 48 Scottish kings (including Duncan, killed by Macbeth), 8 Norwegian kings and 4 Irish kings, though none of these is marked. More recently John Smith, the former Labour Party leader, was buried here but the locals regretted the publicity and nearby graves were damaged by the new influx of visitors. If you do visit the graveyard, please show respect for all the graves. There are several B&Bs and restaurants near the Iona ferry landing, though these are more costly than those on Mull.

From Iona, backtrack the 20 miles to Kinloch.

Stage 2: Kinloch-Tobermory

From Kinloch the B8035 climbs a long hill with amazing views over Staffa and Ulva. It is then a steep descent to Loch Na Keal, and a roaring freewheel under Ben More. The end of the loch at Gruline is wooded and there is plenty of wildlife, including buzzards and wildcats. At this point you could continue for 3 miles on the B8035 to Salen and return to Craignure down the A849.

However, the little B8073 follows the west coast of Mull north from Gruline and is fantastic. At first there are beautiful birch woods and views over to Ben More, then there is the magical isle of Ulva. Ring the bell to summon a ferry and cross to the tearoom which does home baking, as well as selling oysters which are farmed locally. From Ulva continue north past Eas Fors waterfall, which plunges spectacularly into the sea. The road here has steep hills but the wonderful scenery makes the heavy going worthwhile.

There is nothing much on the road to Calgary in the way of teashops. It is a marvellous quiet road, the beach at Calgary is absolutely beautiful, and the Dovecote Restaurant is very welcome.

From Calgary via Dervaig (passing Mull Little Theatre) to Tobermory, the road is quite hilly, with some steep gradients, but it's not far. Tobermory itself is a lovely town built round a harbour. Caledonian Macbrayne operates ferries from the pier to the Ardnamurchan Peninsula. Main Street, with its pretty colour-washed buildings, goes round the bay and everything is there, including some good shops, a bank, a launderette and a post office.

Tobermory means 'Mary's Well' in Gaelic. The town was built in 1787 by the British Fisheries Society and is on an excellent natural harbour. However, this did not help a Spanish galleon, the *Florida*, which sank in the bay in 1588 with a reputed cargo of gold bullion. While this has been sought by divers, no treasure has ever been found.

After the exquisite west coast route, the road back to Craignure via Salen is less spectacular, but in bad weather it is more sheltered. It is fine for cycling but locals moan about the A848 being the worst A road in Britain.

Route 16: Skye

See Fact Sheet 12

Stage 1: Kyle of Lochalsh-Dunvegan

The best way to get to Skye has to be across the tiny romantic ferry at Glenelg (see Route 17), but as most people arrive at Kyle of Lochalsh that is where this route starts.

The new Skye Bridge has been controversial with locals, partly because the tolls are the highest in Britain. Bikes, however, cross for free. The bridge also means that Skye is no longer a true island, and the romance that idea generated has suffered. Skye has always had a huge appeal, from its association with Flora Macdonald who rowed the fugitive Bonnie Prince Charlie (see feature on page 77) to Skye. This area is also where Gavin Maxwell wrote his classic book about otters, *Ring of Bright Water*.

The south part of Skye has limited appeal for cyclists. The road to Sligachan has some nice views but it is a bit fast and truck-infested. Broadford has a youth hostel but little charm. At Luib there is a tea-room and a croft museum in a traditional black house which had a lovely peat fire in the grate when I visited.

The Cuillins are a magnificent series of mountains but access is by foot, not bike. From Sligachan take the westbound A863 to Drynoch Here, a branch to the left leads to the Talisker whisky distillery, Glenbrittle and Portnalong bunkhouse, all on separate but rewarding culs-de-sac.

➤ 74

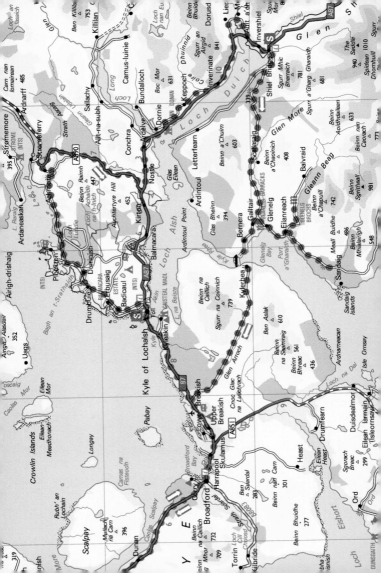

Fact Sheet 12

Skye

Skye is Scotland's largest island and is suitable for good energetic cycling, but be warned, there are lots of other cyclists. The main routes are busy by island standards with vehicular traffic. The best parts are the western coast by Dunvegan, and the northern Trotternish Peninsula, with the Old Man of Storr and the mean and moody Quiraing.

➤ **OS Maps 23, 32**

➤ **Tourist Information Offices (Summer only)**
Broadford, tel. 01471 822361
Uig, Ferry Terminal, tel. 01470 542404
Kyle of Lochalsh, tel. 01599 534276 (mainland)

➤ **Rail**
Skye is served by two lines which are a trainspotter's dream. The West Highland Line, which terminates at Mallaig after its run from Glasgow Queen Street via Fort William, and the Kyle line to Kyle of Lochalsh from Inverness. Advance booking for bikes is essential as space is strictly limited. Tel. 0345 484950 (enquiries) or 0345 550033 (bookings).

➤ **Ferries**
The ferry between Kyle of Lochalsh and Kyleakin was replaced by the new Skye Bridge in 1995
Mallaig-Armadale, Skye/Uig, Skye-Lochmaddy, North Uist/Uig-Tarbert, Harris Caledonian MacBrayne tel. 01475 650100
The small ferry on the tourist route from Glenelg to Kylerhea is certainly worth a detour. Cattle used to have to swim this passage. Tel. 01599 511302 (summer only).

➤ **Cycle Shops**
Hebridean Pedal Highway, Kyleakin, tel. 01599 534842
Skye Bikes, The Pier, Kyleakin, tel. 01599 534795
Island Cycles, The Green, Portree, tel. 01478 613121
Fairwinds Cycle Hire, Broadford, tel. 01471 822270

➤ **Hostels**
SYHA, Armadale, tel. 01471 844260
SYHA, Kyleakin, tel. 01599 534585
SYHA, Broadford, tel. 01471 822442
SYHA, Uig, tel. 01470 542211
SYHA, Glenbrittle, tel. 01478 640278
SYHA, Raasay, tel. 01478 660240
Skye Backpackers, Kyleakin, tel. 01599 534510
The Cliffe, Kyleakin, tel. 01599 534778

Fossil Bothy, Lower Breakish, tel. 01471 822644 (day)/822297
Dun Flodigarry Hostel, Staffin, tel. 01470 552212
Portree Backpackers, 2 Douglas Street, Portree, tel. 01478 613332
Croft Bunkhouse, Portnalong, tel. 01478 640250
Glen Hinneddale Bunkhouse, Snizort, near Uig, tel. 01470 542293

➤ **Banks**
Royal Bank of Scotland, Bank Street, Portree, tel. 01478 612822
Bank of Scotland, Broadford, tel. 01471 822211

➤ **Launderettes**
These can be found at the SYHA at Kyleakin as well as at the Dun Flodigarry
Hostel at Staffin and the Croft Bunkhouse at Portnalong.

The road to Dunvegan is hilly with good views. At Lonmore the little
B884 leads to Colbost on the Duirinish Peninsula. There is a museum
celebrating Angus Macaskill, the world's largest man, born in 1825.
He worked in freak shows. The Croft Museum also has an illegal still,
just in case anyone feels like learning how to make their own whisky.
The nearby Three Chimneys Restaurant, tel. 01470 511258, is highly
recommended. On the road to Boreraig you can visit the
MacCrimmon Piping Centre, devoted to a family of pipers who ran a
piping college for over 250 years. (Admission charge.) At Glendale
further west there is an eccentric toy museum.

Dunvegan Castle, at the junction of the A850 and A863, is the 700-
year-old seat of the Clan Macleod and one of Skye's most popular
attractions. The current clan chief, John Macleod, is an actor and
singer. The house is open to the public and the most famous relic is a
silk cloth, the Fairy Flag, which has magic properties reputed to have
bailed out the Macleods. They got three wishes, two of which have
been used. Dr Johnson visited Dunvegan in 1773, during a wet week.
The castle has a visitor centre and tearoom. (Admission charge.)

Stage 2: Dunvegan-Staffin

The route between Dunvegan and Loch Snizort runs through a series
of crofting townships. About 4 miles along the B886 is the Stein Inn,
tel. 01470 592362, the oldest licensed premises on Skye. The hilly
road gives great views over the Minch to Harris and is not too busy.
Edinbain has a pottery which is open to visitors. At Skeabost there is
a very large hotel which does teas with aplomb.

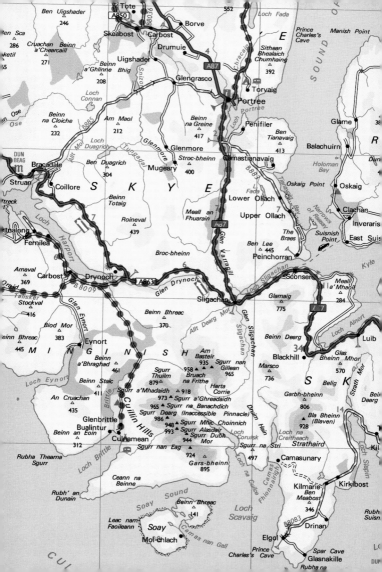

North of Skeabost is the wonderful Trotternish Peninsula. The west coast is spectacular with views over the Atlantic. At Uig the route goes over the moody, dramatic road which rejoices in the name of The Quiraing. The road runs in a deep valley between spectacular hills. The descent to Staffin is very steep. Staffin itself is great. There is a really good independent hostel, as well as the Oyster-catcher Tearoom, which does splendid home baking.

If you are put off by the climb over the Quiraing, the coast road takes you past the Skye Museum of Island Life, a collection of thatched croft houses and old agricultural tools. (Admission charge.) Pass ruined Duntulm Castle, erstwhile seat of the Macdonalds, and continue to Flodigarry House Hotel and another hostel. The hotel is reputedly where Flora Macdonald lived, and is nowadays good for partying on Saturday nights.

From Staffin head south on the A855, enjoying the views across to Raasay. The geological formations which rise to the Old Man of Storr, a rocky needle, and form the spectacular cliffs are composed of basalt bearing down on soft sandstones. Further on, Loch Leathan is a good place for a picnic.

Portree is the capital of Skye and has a picturesque harbour, as well as a number of decent shops and a swimming pool, tel. 01478 612655. Local hotels often have ceilidhs – ask at the Tourist Information Office for details – and for a further cultural fix, visit the Aros Heritage Centre with its costumed figures and audiovisual presentations. (Admission charge.) For arts events and exhibitions, there's the An Tuireann Centre, tel. 01478 613306.

From Portree, the A87 goes the 9 uneventful miles back to Sligachan.

BONNIE PRINCE CHARLIE

Visitors to Scotland are unlikely to escape without seeing houses and caves where Bonnie Prince Charlie stayed and battlefields where his Jacobite followers fought. The term Jacobite comes from the name James, as some people favoured James VII as monarch over the ruling Hanoverian family, and the uprisings continued from 1689 until 1746. Charles Edward Stuart – Bonnie Prince Charlie – was the grandson of James VII and anxious to gain the thrones of Scotland and England.

The '45 Rebellion began when Charles and a small party of followers landed from France, first on Eriskay in the Hebrides then at Loch nan Uamh near Arisaig. He raised the Jacobite standard at Glenfinnan in August 1745. In a few weeks he had inflicted several defeats on Government troops and had got as far south as Derby in the English Midlands. Some historians believe that he could have taken London but instead he withdrew to Scotland, where he was finally defeated at Culloden, near Inverness, by the Hanoverian army commanded by the Duke of Cumberland on 16 April 1746, the last battle to be fought on British soil.

After Culloden, Bonnie Prince Charlie was pursued by the Hanoverian Redcoats until he managed to flee to France on 20 September 1746 and then on to Italy, where he finished his days in drunkenness and debauchery.

The disastrous defeat at Culloden led to the cultural cleansing of the Highlands and the dismantling of the clan structure. Playing the bagpipes, eating haggis and wearing the kilt were all banned. This in turn paved the way for the Highland Clearances, when many Scots were driven from their land.

Despite his ultimately unsuccessful quest, Bonnie Prince Charlie retains a huge amount of affection among the Scots, and visitors from around the world, to this day.

Route 17: Glenelg, southern Skye & Plockton
See Fact Sheet 13 and first Map for Route 16

Start at the foot of Glen Shiel in the shadow of the craggy Five Sisters of Kintail. These are particularly fine-looking mountains.

The road climbs quite steeply to Bealach Ratagan, following an old military road, to a summit of 1112 ft – a demanding climb. There is a great freewheel down the other side to Glenelg, where the Glenelg Inn, tel. 01599 522273, is one of the most pleasant hostelries in Scotland, with good food, open fires and heavenly scenery. Curiously, Dr Samuel Johnson made the place famous by complaining about its harshness and lack of amenities on his journey through the Highlands with Boswell.

➤ 80

Fact Sheet 13 ·

Southern Skye & Kyle

The Skye Bridge has removed some of the mystique of going over the sea to Skye. But this alternative route – possible only in summer when the tiny ferry runs – is undoubtedly the best road to the isles, going via Glenelg, where some remarkably well-preserved brochs are worth a detour. The route crosses back to the mainland via the new bridge and visits the conservation village of Plockton, made famous recently by the TV programme *Hamish Macbeth*. It then runs past Eilean Donan Castle, one of the most picturesque, and most familiar, in Scotland.

➤ **OS Maps 24, 25, 33**

➤ **Tourist Information Offices (Summer only)**
Shiel Bridge, tel. 01599 511264
Broadford, Skye, tel. 01471 822361
Kyle of Lochalsh, tel. 01599 534276

➤ **Rail**
There are stations at Plockton and Kyle of Lochalsh on the line from Kyle of Lochalsh to Inverness.

➤ **Ferry**
Glenelg-Kylerhea (April-October)
Tel. 01599 511302

➤ **Cycle Shops**
Fairwinds Cycle Hire, Broadford, tel. 01471 822270
Skye Bikes, The Pier, Kyleakin, tel. 01599 534795

➤ **Hostels**
SYHA, Ratagan, tel. 01599 511243
SYHA, Kyleakin, tel. 01599 534585
Skye Backpackers' Hostel, Kyleakin, tel. 01599 534510
The Cliffe, Kyleakin, tel. 01599 534778
Fossil Bothy, Lower Breakish, tel. 01471 822644 (day)/297 (evening)

➤ **Banks**
In Broadford and Kyle of Lochalsh.

➤ **Launderette**
Sutherland's Garage, Broadford, tel. 01471 822225

The road branches at the cemetery. The right fork goes to the ferry, while the other fork goes south past the pub and on towards the Glenelg Brochs. It is highly recommended that you take this detour up Gleann Beag to visit these remarkable structures. The Dun Telve Broch is over 30 ft high and it is possible to go inside. (Free.) Further up the glen is the Dun Trodden Broch, which is less perfectly preserved but still of interest. Brochs were built by the Picts, and occur only in Scotland. Their use is mysterious: they could not have been effective defensive structures as they are easy to climb.

The author Gavin Maxwell, who wrote *Ring of Bright Water*, lived in Sandaig further south. The house where he lived was burned down but many of the otters still survive. Maxwell was not as sentimental an animal lover as his books might suggest. He started a shark fishery on Soay, off Skye. Basking sharks – Scotland's largest fish – are easy to harpoon, but they deserted the area when he started commercial hunting and the venture failed. However, the otters which he loved have thrived and the basking sharks have now returned to the area.

The route to Skye via Kylerhea is very ancient. Islanders used to swim their cattle across the Kyle Rhea narrows, which are only 500 yd wide, but can be strongly tidal and treacherous to men and animals. The private ferry, which is small and rickety, received a boost from the controversial Skye Bridge, as many people sought a romantic alternative to the concrete span. And the Kylerhea crossing is everything the Romantic could want.

From the ferry the route heads northwest to join up with the busier A87 near Broadford. Turn right and head to Kyleakin to cross back to the mainland. The Skye Bridge has caused controversy on the island and many residents feel bitter about the high toll levels. But it is now firmly established and bicycles travel free, so it's best not to complain. The bridge has complex anti-otter walls and tunnels, as well as other defences, but despite it all the animals continue cheekily to use the bridge.

Kyle of Lochalsh is the terminus for the wonderful railway from Inverness. The cycle route follows the railway line north along the coast to the magical little village of Plockton. The bay is full of sailing boats and the waterfront is lined with palm trees which thrive in the mild Gulf Stream weather. There are various hotels, the best being the Haven Hotel, tel. 01599 544233, which has good food. There are no hostels here but this isn't a problem as there are plenty of B&Bs.

The TV series *Hamish Macbeth* was filmed here, and Plockton is one of the places that really is as good as it looks. I covered a story about two rival owners of Highland cows who both claimed that his was the true beast that appeared in the opening credits to this eccentric programme. Such is the stuff of Highland village life, I guess.

From Plockton continue east along Loch Carron and join the A890 south of Achmore. Head south to Auchtertyre and go east on the A87. Caution is advisable as cars do drive fast on this road.

After about 3 miles cross the Dornie Bridge and witness one of Scotland's real fairy-tale sights – Eilean Donan Castle. The appearance is a bit deceptive as the castle has been completely restored in the 20thC by one George Mackie Watson for Colonel Macrae-Gilstrap. The castle was built in the 13thC but was blown up by the English during the 1719 Jacobite Rising. It remained deserted for the next two centuries.

If you are yearning to get off the main road, a back road runs parallel to the main road from Dornie as far as Inverinate. It is then a short run back to Shiel Bridge.

Route 18: Orkney

See Fact Sheet 14

The ferry crossing from Scrabster to Burwick on South Ronaldsay crosses the wild Pentland Firth, one of the most notorious tidal races around Britain. It is refreshing after the disappointing John o' Groats to find the crossing so adventurous. It is hard not to feel sorry for the poor souls who walk the length of Britain to drink their champagne at this northernmost point. Orkney is a collection of islands but the locals like to refer to the biggest island as Mainland, which is where the main towns of Kirkwall and Stromness are situated.

Stage 1: Burwick-Kirkwall

At the southeast end of South Ronaldsay is one of the many ancient monuments for which Orkney is famous. The Tomb of the Eagles is a 5000-year-old tomb which was partly excavated by ➤ 83

Fact Sheet 14

Orkney

The Orkney Islands are quite different in feel to Shetland. The land is fertile, with crops growing, and many sheep and cows. The archaeological remains are particularly impressive, although they are not cheap to visit. Tourism here is well developed and all the attractions are signposted. Skara Brae is worth seeing, of course, but was built 5000 years ago and was uncovered by a large storm, so it is hard to see why the admission charges should be so high. The local Orkney cheese is plentiful, described by admirers as being 'clean' and by detractors as being 'like cardboard'.

➤ **OS Maps 5, 6, 7**

➤ **Tourist Information Offices (Summer only)**
Stromness, The Pier Head, tel. 01856 850716

➤ **Ferries**
Scrabster, near Thurso-Stromness, Mainland Orkney.
2-3 services per day.
P&O Scottish Ferries, tel. 01856 850655/01224 572615
John o' Groats-Burwick, South Ronaldsay
A passenger ferry which takes bikes (May-September only). Coach transfers from Thurso railway station and bus connections to Inverness are available.
John o' Groats Ferries, tel. 01955 611353/342
Invergordon-Kirkwall
A new overnight service which avoids a long cycle up the east coast.
Price includes cabin and meals.
Orcargo, tel. 01856 873838
Orkney Island Shipping Company, 4 Ayre Road, Kirkwall (Information line, tel. 01426 977170, otherwise tel. 01856 872044) operates inter-island ferries. Island Explorer tickets are available which give unlimited travel for 10 days.

➤ **Airlines**
The main Orkney airport is at Kirkwall. For more information contact British Airways, tel. 0345 222111. The world's shortest scheduled flight – about 2 min – is from Westray to Papa Westray, and is certainly worth doing. Bicycles are allowed on aeroplanes, subject to room being available.

➤ **Buses**
Buses will usually be carried at the driver's discretion, but contact J.D. Peace, Junction Road, Kirkwall, tel. 01856 872866, for more information.

➤ **Cycle Shops**
Brown's Independent Hostel, 45 Victoria Street, Stromness, tel. 01856 850661. Bike hire.
Orkney Cycle Hire, 54 Dundas Street, Stromness, tel. 01856 850255

Paterson's, Tankerness Lane, Kirkwall, tel. 01856 873097. Bike hire.
Eviedale Centre, in the northeast of Mainland Orkney, tel. 01856 751254.
A range of sports activities, including bike hire, and a café with an open fire.

➤ **Hostels**
SYHA, Kirkwall, Old Scapa Road, tel. 01856 872243
SYHA, Stromness, Hellihole Road, tel. 01856 850589
Also youth hostels at Rackwick on Hoy, contact Orkney Education
Department, tel. 01856 873535, and on Papa Westray, tel. 01857 4267, which
also has bike hire.
Brown's Independent Hostel, 45 Victoria Street, Stromness, tel. 01856 850661
Wheems Bothy, Eastside, South Ronaldsay, tel. 01856 850661
Herston Hikers' Hostel, South Ronaldsay. Contact Mr Annal, tel. 01856
831208. Cheap, with a coal fire.
Evie Hostel, tel. 01856 751208, in the northeast of Mainland Orkney, opposite
the Isle of Rousay.

➤ **Banks**
Clydesdale Bank, 3 Broad Street, Kirkwall, tel. 01856 873237
Royal Bank of Scotland, Victoria Street, Stromness, tel. 01856 850217
Bank of Scotland, Victoria Street, Stromness, tel. 01856 850238

➤ **Launderettes**
47 Albert Street, Kirkwall, tel. 01856 872982
Ferry Road, Stromness, tel. 01856 850904
Kirkwall Youth Hostel has a washing machine and drier.

local farmer Ron Simison, who lives close by and does tours, tel.
01856 831339. (Admission charge.) You get to handle Stone-Age
tools and even skulls!

Backtrack through Burwick and follow signs for St Margaret's Hope.
The cycling is pleasant and not very hilly, passing through fertile
farmland. In the village are a tearoom, the Coachhouse, as well as the
Wireless Museum and Old Smiddy Museum. (Admission charge.)
Bunkhouse accommodation is also available.

Continue on to Burray across the first causeway and find the Fossil
Museum, tel. 01856 731255, with a tearoom and some beautiful
gems. Burray also has a working boatyard.

The islands south of Mainland are linked by causeways built following
the sinking of HMS *Royal Oak* in August 1939 by a German U-boat
which slipped through the defences. Churchill ordered the barriers to

be built by Italian prisoners of war. Apart from the causeways, another legacy of the Italians is the hauntingly beautiful Italian Chapel, constructed out of a Nissen hut, with frescoes and inscriptions which explain its construction. The chapel is open all the time and is on the island of Lamb Holm.

From here cross onto Mainland Orkney, leaving behind Scapa Flow. St Mary's is a quiet little village. At Graemeshall there is a collection of remarkable antiques gathered together by Norrie Wood. He was in the national news for owning a series of statues, *The Three Graces*, which he salvaged from Inverness Council.

The approaches to Kirkwall are unexciting farming country, but as you get to the outskirts you pass the Highland Park Distillery, tel. 01856 874619, with audiovisual presentations and drams of 12-year-old nectar. (Free.)

The cultural life of Kirkwall is reasonably vibrant. Music clubs meet in the Ayre Hotel on Wednesday and the Community Centre on Thursday. The magnificent St Magnus' Cathedral, completed in 1137, is very pleasing on the eye, with its red sandstone walls. It was founded by Earl Rognvald, and is Norman in style. Until 1472 this was part of the Norwegian diocese.

Across the road is the 12thC Bishop's Palace and the Earl's Palace (admission charges), built in 1600 by Earl Patrick Stewart, a local tyrant with a taste for fine Renaissance architecture. Nearby is Tankerness House Museum, which explores the social and cultural history of Orkney. This is in a restored merchant's mansion, built in 1574, which also has a nice garden. (Admission charge.) In Laing Street is the oldest public library in Scotland, founded in 1683.

Stage 2: Kirkwall-Stromness

Head out of Kirkwall on the A965, following signs to Finstown. Wideford Hill Cairn, dating from 3500 BC, is a chambered tomb a mile from the road. Access is by a trap door. Rennibister Earth House or souterrain is where Iron-Age human bones have been found.

Finstown is rather scenic, at the head of the Bay of Firth. The town is named after an Irish publican, Phin. From here head north on the A966 with views out to Shapinsay. Near Evie the Broch of Gurness is the best-preserved broch (see feature on page 86) in Orkney, and is surrounded by the remains of Iron-Age and later dwellings. There is an interpretative museum. (Admission charge.) Evie is a good place to stay overnight, with two hostels and a café, as well as views of Rousay. Seals and sometimes otters can be seen here.

Continue northwest along the coast. At Birsay the ruined Earl's Palace dates from the 16thC. Close by is the Brough of Birsay, another broch, on an island complete with Viking and Pictish remains, which is accessible at low tide. Birsay was the seat of the Norse strongman Thorfinn the Mighty, who lived from 1009 until 1065.

As you head down the west coast you pass by RSPB bird reserves mainly frequented by wading birds. At the Bay of Skaill, which has sandy beaches, is the world-famous Skara Brae, an amazing group of Stone-Age dwellings with furniture and many artefacts *in situ*, including Neolithic cosmetics. The buildings were buried and preserved in sand until they were exposed by a storm in 1824. (Admission charge.)

From Skara Brae it is worth taking the B9055 past Hestwall between the Lochs of Stenness and Harray. Apart from being very scenic, this takes you past two remarkable Neolithic sites. First is the Ring of Brodgar, an astounding stone circle with 27 stones still standing. Further on are the Standing Stones of Stenness. Turn left on the A965 towards Finstown and after a short distance is Maes Howe, a burial mound dating from 2750 BC which was opened in 1861. The Vikings had been there first and left 12thC graffiti. From Maes Howe, backtrack on the A965 to Stromness.

Stromness is a quiet and attractive little town. Once a thriving whaling station and outpost of the Hudson Bay Trading Company, Stromness clusters round its Main Street which is paved with local flagstone. The Pier Arts Centre houses 20thC art in a converted 19thC building, while Stromness Museum, established in 1837, is south of the main ferry pier. There are interesting exhibits on the scuttling of the German High Fleet in Scapa Flow in 1919. (Admission charge.) The town has a hostel and other services, including a bike shop. It also has a ferry that links with Scrabster on the Scottish mainland, as well as Shetland.

From Stromness many visitors travel to Hoy, a hilly island famous for its Old Man of Hoy, a spectacular sea stack surrounded by puffins and guillemots. There is good walking but cycling is limited.

BROCHS

Brochs are enigmatic buildings which are unique to Scotland. In total there are about 600 broch sites throughout the northwest of Scotland, plus in the Hebrides, Shetland and Orkney. There are well-known brochs at Glenelg, near Kyle of Lochalsh, Gurness in Orkney and Mousa in Shetland. All brochs take a tall tower form with one door and no windows, and date from 100 BC to AD 100. They have no obvious use, but it may well be that they were defensive structures built to show the status of the community. Many occupy fine agricultural sites.

◆ Route 19: Shetland

(◆) See Fact Sheet 15

Cycling in Shetland is very rewarding, but the islands are surprisingly big and there is a lot of backtracking involved. None of the routes are totally satisfactory. Much of the islands are peaty and can be rather bleak, as well as suffering atrocious weather. The locals also share a sense of humour with their Scandinavian neighbours. One small boy, asked if it always rains in Shetland, said, 'How should I know? I'm only eight.' However, when the weather is good it is magical, with 19 hours of sun in June and no darkness – just a twilight known as the 'simmer dim'.

Stage 1: Lerwick-Walls

Lerwick is a bustling little town, with a harbour which attracts fishermen from Scandinavia and the Faeroes. In winter the town is invaded by a flotilla of factory ships from former Eastern Bloc countries known collectively as the Klondykers. They follow the shoals of herring and mackerel which migrate through these waters. While this trade has continued for many years, indeed centuries, there have recently been problems with these ships not paying their bills or not being seaworthy and going onto rocks. Many of the crews work in poor conditions, but can make good money. The islanders still welcome the Russians, partly from tradition and partly because the trade value to Shetland is huge.

Shetland fiddle music is famous and worth seeking out. The Lounge Bar in Mounthooly Street has sessions some evenings. The late Tammy Anderson is credited with recording much of the Shetland fiddle repertoire, while Ali Bain is now its most famous performer. There is a Shetland Folk Festival in late April/early May and a fiddle festival in October which are recommended. Worth visiting is the Shetland Museum on Lower Hillhead, which details the social history of the islands. (Free.) You should also visit the Clickhimin Broch, a fortified Iron-Age site with a 17 ft-high broch, in south Lerwick. (Free.) On a prosaic level, the site is also close to the local Presto supermarket.

The route leaves Lerwick on a steep climb and soon there are views out over Bressay. The little town of Tingwall has a museum of agriculture, which explains Shetland crofting life. (Admission charge.) Nearby at Loch Tingwall is the Law Ting Holm, thought to have been a meeting place for a Norse parliament. Head west through Whiteness and Hjaaltasteyn, where there is a jewellery shop and tearoom. The route is fairly hilly but the long sea lochs create plenty of fine views. At Walls there is a swimming pool, chippie, pub, a ferry to Foula (one of the remotest inhabited islands in Britain) and various historic monuments, such as the Staneydale Neolithic Settlement. Walls also boasts a museum of knitting.

Stage 2: Walls-Unst

Retrace your route back to Bixter and head north to the atmospheric village of Voe on the B9071 and Brae on the A970. Brae is close to the Sullom Voe oil terminal, which has transformed the islands' economy. The nearby Busta House Hotel is highly recommended. North of Brae there is a standing stone close to Mavis Grind, a narrow isthmus over which Vikings dragged their boats. The north part of Mainland, Northmaven, is remote but well worth exploring. Past Hillswick at Eshaness are spectacular cliffs and a blow hole which channels waves into a spout. Also nearby is a beach where semi-precious stones can be found.

The most northerly part of Shetland, Muckle Flugga, is not accessible. However, the islands of Yell and Unst are spectacular. Yell is much maligned as being boring, but it has its own quiet charm. It is useful, however, to book accommodation in advance. There is a tearoom at Burravoe and another at Gutcher. From Gutcher take the ferry to Unst and continue north through Haroldswick to Hermaness ➤ 89

Shetland

Fact Sheet 15 . . . .

The Shetland Islands are remote even from Scotland, and their inhabitants are proud of their Scandinavian links. Cycling here can be a fantastic experience, but the northern latitude means that cold windy weather is common. Facilities are sparse and the islands are deceptively large. A level of pre-planning helps. Camping in Shetland in poor weather can be miserable. Warm clothes and good waterproofs are needed, even in summer.

➤ OS Maps 1, 2, 3, 4

➤ **Tourist Information Office**
Lerwick (see Fact Sheet on page 65)

➤ **Ferries**
Aberdeen-Lerwick
P&O, PO Box 5, Jamieson's Quay, Aberdeen, tel. 01224 572615.
Holmsgarth Terminal, Lerwick, tel. 01595 695252.
For details of ferries within Shetland, contact Shetland Islands Ferries, tel. 01595 692024.

➤ **Airlines**
There is an airport at Sumburgh at the southern tip of Mainland, with bus links to Lerwick. For more information, contact British Airways, tel. 0345 222111. In practice, bicycles can be carried, but telephone in advance for confirmation.

➤ **Buses**
Bus drivers in Shetland often allow bikes to be carried, subject to available room. For more details, contact John Leask and Son, Lerwick, tel. 01595 693162.

➤ **Cycle Shop**
Eric Brown, 68 Commercial Road, Lerwick, tel. 01595 693733. Raleigh dealer.

➤ **Hostels**
It is recommended that you call the Tourist Information Office in advance to arrange accommodation. For low-cost accommodation try staying in a Bod, one of a series of camping barns which can also be booked through the Tourist Information Office.
SYHA, Isleburgh House, Lerwick, tel. 01595 692114. Newly refitted.
Gardiesfauld Independent Youth Hostel, Uyeasound, tel. 01957 755298, or contact the warden, tel. 01957 755311. Cheap self-catering with masses of room, so you will almost certainly get in.
Baltasound Hotel, Unst, tel. 01957 711334. Fairly pricey for chalet-type accommodation. This is the most northerly hotel.

Bods (camping barns) are located at Nesbister on Whiteness Voe, Sail Loft at Voe and Grieve House at Whalsay, as well as Johnnie Notions (named after the inventor John Williamson) at Eshaness on northwest Mainland.

➤ **Banks**
Clydesdale Bank, 106 Commercial Street, Lerwick, tel. 01595 695664
Royal Bank of Scotland, 117 Commercial Street, Lerwick, tel. 01595 692624
Royal Bank of Scotland, Scalloway, tel. 01595 880475

➤ **Launderette**
Lerwick Laundry, 36 Market Street, Lerwick, tel. 01595 693043

Nature Reserve. This is a fair walk, but the seabird colonies are amazing. Beware of the aggressive Great Skua, known locally as Bonxies, which divebomb like the Red Baron. They do skim you, and a big bird could potentially do you no good. There is method in this madness though, as they are trying to protect their chicks in the nests on the clifftop. At Uveasound there is a youth hostel and nearby is Britain's most northerly castle at Muness. From here return to Lerwick. As the ferries interlink and assume you are travelling by car, if you cycle you will miss every ferry by 10 min. Instead, take the coach south; taking a bike should be no problem.

South of Lerwick are some of Shetland's finest visitor attractions. The outstandingly well-preserved Mousa Broch on a little island near Sandwick can be visited on tours organized through the Tourist Information Office. On the west side of Shetland a couple of miles south off the B9122 is the lovely St Ninian's Isle, linked to Mainland by a sandy spit, where a treasure trove of silver was discovered in the 1950s.

At the south of Mainland near Sumburgh Airport is the Jarlshof Settlement, where remains of occupation through the Stone Age, Bronze Age, Viking era and later can be traced. (Admission charge.) Nearby on Sumburgh Head the remains of the oil tanker *Braer* can be seen. The vessel went aground in January 1993 and caused a serious pollution incident.

THE GREAT GLEN & LOCH NESS

The Great Glen is a deep rift valley with a series of long, freshwater lochs, the most famous of which is Loch Ness. The glen has a huge – one could say monstrous – attraction for thousands of visitors each year, and at its southern end is Ben Nevis, Britain's highest mountain. To the west of Fort William, the main centre hereabouts, is Moidart, remote, beautiful and far less touristy.

➤ **Route 20**
Moidart Loop
♦ (♦) Easy to moderate. 101/119 miles.

➤ **Route 21**
Great Glen Cycle Route
♦♦ Moderate, with some steep, rough, off-road sections. 69 miles.

➤ **Route 22**
Three Lochs
♦ Easy, with some hills. 21 miles.

➤ **Route 23**
Beauly Firth Loop
♦ Easy. 26 miles.

➤ **Rail**
There are services from the Scottish Central Belt and from England to Inverness. Services also operate from Inverness to Aberdeen, Kyle of Lochalsh and the Far North of Scotland, including Wick and Thurso. For more information, tel. 01463 238924. Trains operate to Fort William via Crianlarich from Glasgow Queen Street. For more information, tel. 01397 703791.

➤ **Ferry**
Corran Ferry, near Onich, south of Fort William
C.F. Ltd, tel. 01855 811243

➤ **Cycle Tour Organizers**
Offbeat Bikes, 117 High Street, Fort William, tel. 01397 704008. Hire, repair and a shop giving advice on local routes.
Bespoke Highland Tours operates tours in Moidart. See page 227.

➤ **Tourist Information Offices (Open all year)**
Fort William, Cameron Square, tel. 01397 703781
Inverness, Castle Wynd, tel. 01463 234353

➤ **Other Useful Numbers**

Caledonian Canal Manager, British Waterways, Muirtown Wharf, Inverness, tel. 01463 233140

Forestry Enterprise, Fort Augustus, tel. 01320 366322, and Torlundy, Fort William, tel. 01397 702184

➤ **Special Events**

The Nevis River Race takes place at Fort William in August, and there are the Lochaber Games and Inverness Highland Games in July.

Route 20: Moidart Loop

See Fact Sheets 16 and 17

The route goes through some beautiful, unspoilt scenery. There are few organized tourist attractions and you shouldn't rely on regular tearooms – it's just you, the sea, the sky and the odd eagle.

Start in Fort William and head south about 10 miles on the A82 to Corran Ferry (all year, tel. 01855 811243) across Loch Linnhe. Alternatively, park at Corran Ferry. Follow the A861 south to Inversanda and continue to Strontian. Here you will find a tearoom, as well as a fish and chip shop near the police station. A leaflet available from the Tourist Information Office details mountain bike trails and walks in Ariundle Woods just north on the Polloch road. Here are wonderful mature oak woods, plus birch and rowans. Cosy Knits sells woollens as well as being a pottery and a tearoom.

From Strontian head west along the banks of Loch Sunart for 12 miles to Salen. This is a beautiful road through stunning scenery. At Salen you could continue to Kilchoan on the Ardnamurchan Peninsula and cross to Mull to join Route 15. The Salen Hotel has a nice open fire and serves good sandwiches.

Head north on the A861 to Acharacle, a scattered township which is a good place to find a B&B. It's best to book ahead at Strontian Tourist Information Office. About 3 miles from Acharacle, up a minor road and in a fantastic location, is romantic, ruined Castle Tioram. The castle is accessible by a causeway at low tide, with signs warning you not to get stuck if the tide comes in. The castle's ➤ 94

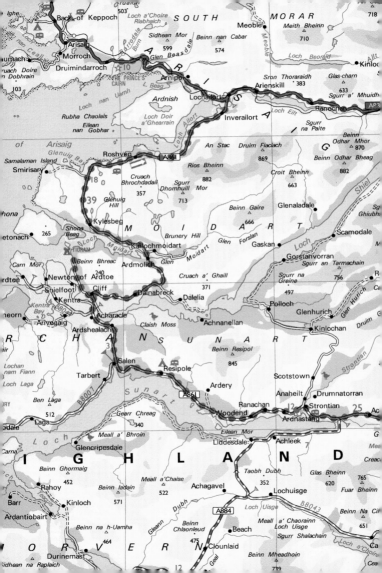

Fort William

Fact Sheet 16 ·

Fort William attracts many tourists and has a wide range of accommodation, much situated on the side of Loch Linnhe. It is also one of the wettest towns in Scotland. Yes, it's that wet! However, as a result the scenery is spectacular and Ben Nevis, Britain's highest mountain, is nearby.

➤ **OS Maps 40, 41, 49**

➤ **Tourist Information Offices (Summer only)**
Strontian, Moidart, tel. 01967 402131
Spean Bridge, tel. 01397 712576

➤ **Cycle Shops**
Offbeat Bikes, 117 High Street, tel. 01397 704008/705825. Bike hire, repairs and advice on local routes.

➤ **Hostels**
SYHA, Glen Nevis, 3 miles up the glen, tel. 01397 702336
The Old Smiddy, Station Road, Corpach, tel. 01397 772467
Ben Nevis Bunkhouse, Achintee Farm, Glen Nevis, tel. 01397 702240
Fort William Backpackers, Alma Road, Fort William, tel. 01397 700711
Inchree Bunkhouse, Onich, near Corran Ferry, tel. 01855 821287

➤ **Banks**
Bank of Scotland, 62 High Street, tel. 01397 703497
Royal Bank of Scotland, 6 High Street, tel. 01397 705191

➤ **Launderette**
Croit Anna Hotel, on A82 just south of Fort William, tel. 01397 702268

massive walls are 13thC and there is also a later tower house, which was burnt down in 1715 during the Jacobite wars.

Back on the main road, continue through Kinlochmoidart, with the select Kinacarra Restaurant (booking essential, tel. 01967 431238), where tea is also served during the day. Further on is the Glenuig Inn, tel. 01687 470219, by Lochailort, with fantastic views over to Rhum and Eigg. This is a super pub with bunkhouse accommodation, a folk music tradition and excellent beer. If you want to catch some folk music or a dance, ring the hotel for details and book accommodation in advance.

Moidart

Fact Sheet 17

This area is attractive precisely because it is so remote and rather hard to get to. There is little in the way of services, and it is therefore advisable to book accommodation in advance. The pub at Glenuig was wonderful when I cycled past – full of hairy musicians and children dancing around.

➤ **OS Maps 40, 41**

➤ **Tourist Information Office (Summer only)**
Strontian, tel. 01967 402131

➤ **Ferries**
Arisaig-Rhum and Eigg
Arisaig Marina, tel. 01687 450219
Mallaig-Inverie, Knoydart
Bruce Watt Cruises, The Pier, Mallaig, tel. 01687 462320
Mallaig-Armadale, Skye
Caledonian Macbrayne, tel. 01475 650100

➤ **Cycle Shops**
There are no cycle shops on the route. Those listed below are the nearest.
Bespoke, The Bothy, Camusdarach, Arisaig, tel. 01687 450272
Offbeat Bikes, 117 High Street, Fort William, tel. 01397 704008/ 705825

➤ **Accommodation**
Glenuig Inn, tel. 01687 470219. Cheap bunkhouse.
Glenfinnan House Hotel, near the Glenfinnan Monument, tel. 01397 722235

In another 8 miles, at Lochailort, is the busier A830. Some traffic goes to Skye via Mallaig, and there's always a few people rushing for the ferry, so take extra care. A little detour northwest is worth doing. About 3 miles along the A830 towards Mallaig by Arisaig House on the banks of Loch nan Uamh is the place where Bonnie Prince Charlie landed and also some caves where he hid. I tried to persuade Prince Michael of Albany, who claims to be the heir to the Stuart throne, to stay in this cave as part of the 250th anniversary celebrations of the Jacobite Uprisings. Unfortunately, the prince felt unable to follow the example of his famous ancestor and brave the chill of a Highland night.

CHAPTER 5

Despite this, the original and 'Bonnie' Jacobite prince continues to hold a great fascination for tourists. The route east of Lochailort on the A830 passes the Glenfinnan Monument, built in 1815 and commemorating the Raising of the Standard by Bonnie Prince Charlie on 19 August 1745. This place has wide appeal to coach tour operators and Jacobite re-enactment enthusiasts, but is shunned by more discerning tourists. A National Trust visitor centre has displays on Bonnie Prince Charlie's life and times. (Admission charge.)

Beyond Glenfinnan there are two choices. Either continue along the busy A830 back to Fort William, or at the head of Loch Eil take the quiet A861 along the loch's south side back to Corran Ferry.

Route 21: Great Glen Cycle Route

See Fact Sheets 16 and 18

The route through the Great Glen is a favourite with tourists, but unfortunately there is limited scope for cycling on quiet back roads in the area. However, a Great Glen Cycle Route has been devised through the Forestry Commission property to allow people to cycle off-road. This route is not suitable for light road bikes; mountain bikes and touring bikes with heavier tyres are ideal. Even so, sections of busy road are still used, so be careful. The amount of traffic on these stretches unfortunately means that the route is of limited suitability for family cycling.

From Fort William follow the A82 northwards, then turn west on the A830 to Mallaig and cycle over the Blar Mhor (Gaelic name for the A82) using the cycle track next to the road. When you reach the Caledonian Canal swing bridge at Banavie, take the right-hand towpath (looking north) past Neptune's Staircase, a spectacular series of nine locks on the Caledonian Canal.

The Caledonian Canal is 60 miles long and links several lochs in the glen, including Loch Ness. Designed by Thomas Telford, it was built to enable shipping to avoid the notorious Pentland Firth and was opened in 1822. It has 29 locks and is still used by fishing boats and yachts. At Lochy Bridge is 13thC Inverlochy Castle, now a crumbling ruin with a moat.

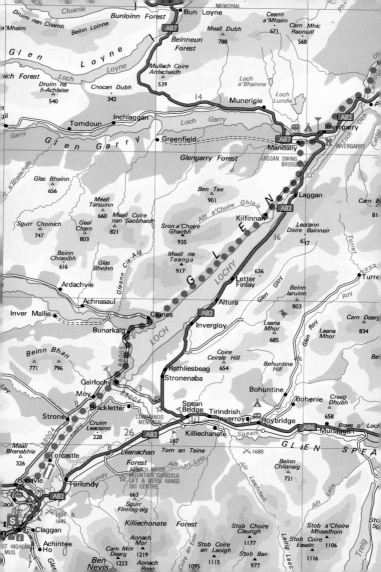

Loch Ness

Fact Sheet 18 . . . .

The Great Glen Cycle Route has been organized by the Forestry Commission and employees of the Caledonian Canal. It works reasonably well, although it is incomplete and rather bitty. The area gets a lot of tourists and it can seem a bit impersonal. However, the alternative route on the south shore of Loch Ness is wonderful.

➤ OS Maps 26, 34, 41

➤ **Tourist Information Offices (Summer only)**
Spean Bridge, tel. 01397 712576
Fort Augustus, tel. 01320 366367

➤ **Cycle Shops**
Great Glen School of Adventure, Laggan, tel. 01809 501381. Bike hire, restaurant, launderette and chalet accommodation.

➤ **Hostels**
SYHA, Loch Lochy, Laggan Locks, tel. 01809 501239
St Benedict's Abbey Bunkhouse, Fort Augustus, tel. 01320 366233
Loch Ness Backpackers' Lodge, Coiltie Farm, Drumnadrochit,
tel. 01630 450807
Foyers House, Foyers, east shore of Loch Ness, tel. 01456 486405

➤ **Banks**
Bank of Scotland, Fort Augustus, tel. 01320 366297
Bank of Scotland, Drumnadrochit, tel. 01456 450237

➤ **Launderette**
Great Glen School of Adventure, Laggan, tel. 01809 501381

The canal climbs from Banavie to its highest point at Oich Bridge. When you reach Gairlochy, cross the canal bridge and turn north on the B8005 for Clunes. A short (22 miles) and easy loop from Fort William is to take the B8004 along the north bank of the canal from Banavie to Gairlochy and return along the towpath.

The first loch you come to is Loch Lochy, and from Clunes the route is fairly flat, combining forest road and single-track tarmac along the north shore past the Glas Dhoir croft and historic Kilfinnan graveyard. The steep hillsides are rich in wildlife. At Laggan a short section of cycle track avoids the A82 and joins the Craig Liath forest road.

The road climbs to give views over ruined Invergarry Castle and up the Great Glen. At the point where the River Garry joins Loch Oich is the bird-like Raven's Rock. The descent to Mandally is swift and brutal. Turn right and cycle 500 yd, then cross the road bridge on the A82 heading north. Turn left through Invergarry, which has a hotel, tearoom and public toilet.

From Invergarry the route climbs steeply on a specific cycle track with good views of Ben Tee and Craig Liath. At the top, cycle through a mature spruce plantation before joining forest roads for the descent towards Loch Oich, where the route turns north on a special cycle track to Oich Bridge through forests with many viewpoints and stopping places. Where the track joins the A82, head about 100 yd towards the canal bridge and from there take the towpath along the west (left-hand) bank to Fort Augustus.

Fort Augustus was built around 1730 by General Wade, who named it after William Augustus, then aged eight and later the Duke of Cumberland, who finally crushed the Jacobite uprisings at Culloden in 1746. The Benedictine Order has an abbey here which is built on the site of Wade's fort, the land being gifted to the Order by Lord Lovat in 1876. There is a Great Glen Exhibition in the town near the canal. (Admission charge.) Eating establishments and accommodation include the Lovat Arms, tel. 01320 366206, St Benedict's Abbey Bunkhouse, tel. 01320 366233, and the Lock Inn, a canal-side pub.

Leave Fort Augustus on the A82, following signs for Inverness. After 1.5 miles turn north into the forest at Allt na Criche car park and picnic site. There is an opportunity here to stop and admire the views of Loch Ness, Fort Augustus and Cherry Island. Alternatively, swat midges, which are horrible in the summer. Cherry Island is the remains of a crannog, a Neolithic stilt dwelling built on the loch.

The next 7 miles are on mostly undulating forestry road with some steep slopes. There are Douglas fir trees growing to more than 100 ft high. Watch out round here as timber is often being harvested. Through gaps in the trees look out for the Horseshoe Crag on the other side of the loch, a vaguely horseshoe-shaped rock and scree and some fragments of native Scots pine. Descend into Invermoriston.

From Invermoriston the route climbs a steep tarmac road to meet the forestry road. Continue to the viewpoint at Achnaconeran, where there are panoramic views over Loch Ness to the hills beyond.

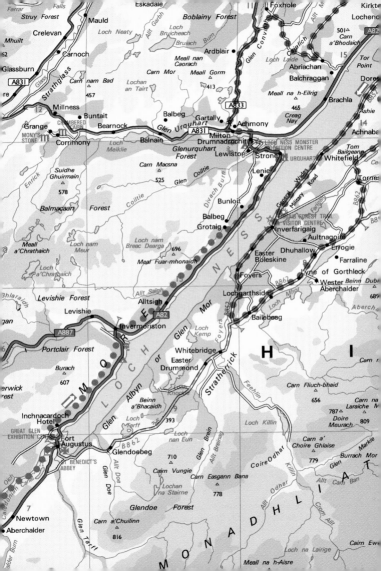

The Glenmoriston estate constructed walks and viewpoints on this hill more than a hundred years ago, and the slab stone seats and rock cave are remnants of this era.

At this point you are in the centre of Nessie-spotting country. Loch Ness Youth Hostel is nearby at the waterside. The route then climbs again quite steeply but at the top you are rewarded with more views and, yes, more forestry roads, and a gentle descent to the bark sheds. Bark from oak trees was harvested here and the tannins extracted for curing leather.

The route at this stage is incomplete at the time of writing, and you should check with Tourist Information Offices for up-to-date details. Currently the route follows the busy A82 for 5 miles. It does, however, pass Drumnadrochit and the splendidly picturesque ruin of Urquhart Castle, which attracts hordes of tourists and has the requisite piper. This is undoubtedly the best place for spotting Nessie. In Drumnadrochit are various cafés and hotels, and two rival Nessie exhibitions. The Official Loch Ness Monster Exhibition is the more interesting. (Admission charge.) It also has the Loch Ness Backpackers' Hostel, tel. 01456 450807.

The official route now heads away from the loch to avoid the busy A82. Again this section is under development and may change. Currently the route follows the A831 west for 2 miles then north on the A833, climbing onto moorland with some lovely lochans, which make good sites for a picnic. Descend Glen Convinth and turn right at the first opportunity, after about 6 miles, then follow signs on back roads to Abriachan. Here there is a sharp junction and the road heads north past a phone box to Blackfold, before descending to rejoin the A82, 3 miles from Inverness. Cross the canal bridge and immediately turn left along Bught Lane, following the riverside to the centre of Inverness.

An alternative route – if you have limited tolerance of forestry plantations – is to break from the route at Fort Augustus and follow the minor roads to the east of Loch Ness (see Route 22).

Route 22: Three Lochs

See Fact Sheet 19 and second Map for Route 21

While the north bank of Loch Ness is busy and poorly served by minor roads, the south bank, by contrast, is a delightful area for cycling, with lots of little roads. The suggested route is a loop based on leaving your car at Dores at the Inverness end of Loch Ness. OS Map 26 is useful for finding alternative routes. However, there are a few short, steep hills.

The first part of the route runs along the south bank of Loch Ness. At Inverfarigaig there is a forest trail plus the remains of an Iron-Age fort, and further on, beyond the Foyers Hotel, is Foyers village. Here there is a wonderful waterfall, an ideal place for a picnic.

Continue through Foyers and turn left up Gleann Liath. After 3 miles turn right to Errogie on Loch Mhor, then keep on the B862 back to Dores. The first lochan, Loch Ceo Glais, is a good place to stop and perhaps to have a swim. Further on near Loch Duntelchaig are some interesting ruins, including a fort, and an ancient field system.

Route 23: Beauly Firth Loop

See Fact Sheet 19 and third Map for Route 21

Inverness Tourist Information Office suggests the following easy tour. It is quite enjoyable apart from crossing the Kessock Bridge.

Leave Inverness on the A862 and follow this west for 7 miles to Inchmore. Near here, at Moniack Castle, tel. 01463 831283, you can sample Scottish birch wine and other delicacies. A right turn here on the B9164 takes you through Kirkhill and back to the A862 at Lovat Bridge. After crossing the bridge, turn right to Beauly.

Beauly is a pukka Highland town which was long the seat of the Lovats. A recent series of deaths has meant that the family has been forced to sell Beaufort Castle to the bus magnate Ann Gloag, co-owner of Stagecoach. The Lovats have often featured in Scottish history. Simon Fraser, a Jacobite known as the 'Old Fox', was executed by the Duke of Cumberland, while another Lord Lovat was a World War I hero and the first chairman of the Forestry Commission.

Continue to Muir of Ord, where you will find the Glen Ord Distillery, tel. 01463 870421. This is the last survivor of an original eight in the area, and was licensed in 1838. It produces the Glen Ord Single Malt, which can be tasted on the guided tour.

Take the A832 east onto the Black Isle for 2.5 miles, then take a right turn on a small road signposted to Redcastle and follow it along the north shore of the Beauly Firth to North Kessock. A footpath up to the A9 allows you to cross the Kessock Bridge back to Inverness. Kessock Bridge is not particularly cycle-friendly.

Fact Sheet 19 .... Inverness

Inverness is known as the 'Capital of the Highlands' and is an important transit point. Although it has a number of interesting attractions, it doesn't really justify its place at the top of the tourist itinerary. However, it does have all the major services, including Marks and Spencer. This is a place to go through rather than a final destination.

➤ **OS Map 26**

➤ **Tourist Information Offices**
Inverness, Castle Wynd, tel. 01463 234353
North Kessock, Ross-shire, tel. 01463 731505
Daviot Wood, A9 south of Inverness, tel. 01463 772203 (summer only)

➤ **Cycle Shops**
Thornton Cycles, 23 Castle Street, tel. 01463 235078. Bike hire.
Bike of Inverness, Grant Street, tel. 01463 225965
The Cycle Works, King Street, tel. 01463 222522

➤ **Hostels**
SYHA, Inverness, 1 Old Edinburgh Road, tel. 01463 231771
Inverness Student Hostel, 8 Culduthel Road, tel. 01463 236556

➤ **Banks**
Bank of Scotland, 9 High Street, tel. 01463 223789
Royal Bank of Scotland, 17 Tomnahurich Street, tel. 01463 236363

➤ **Launderettes**
Inverness Laundries, 14 Grant Street, tel. 01463 239205
Also at 17 Young Street.

THE FAR NORTH

The Far North of Scotland is wonderfully remote, with quiet little roads and breathtaking scenery making for brilliant cycling. However, its remoteness causes logistical problems in getting there. Due to the vagaries of British Rail, one can no longer easily get bikes to and from Inverness. Officially, one bike per train can be carried, which is not much use for couples and groups. Services west to Kyle of Lochalsh and further north to John o' Groats can take 4 bikes per train. The other thing to bear in mind is that there are few tourist facilities in the Far North and this is big country. Be self-sufficient.

➤ **Route 24 (Grand Tour)**
Ullapool-Kylesku-Durness-Lairg-Inverness
◆◆ (◆) Moderate, but strenuous in parts with long hill climbs. 221 miles.

➤ **Route 25**
Achiltibuie & Lochinver
◆◆ Moderate, with some hills. 59 miles.

➤ **Route 26**
Mountain bike route to Achiltibuie
◆◆◆ Strenuous, with some bike carrying. 19 miles.

➤ **Route 27**
Cromarty Loop
◆ Easy. 27 miles.

➤ **Rail**
Inverness is served by trains from the Scottish Central Belt and Aberdeen. There are also services on the Far North Line from Inverness to Thurso and Wick via Lairg. Tel. 0345 484950 (enquiries) or 0345 550033 (bookings).

➤ **Ferry**
Ullapool-Stornoway
Caledonian Macbrayne, tel. 01475 650100

➤ **Cycle Tour Organizers**
Bespoke Highland Tours. See page 227.

➤ **Tourist Information Offices (Open all year)**
Gairloch, Auchtercairn, tel. 01445 712130
Dornoch, The Square, tel. 01862 810400
North Kessock, tel. 01463 731505
Wick, Whitechapel Road, Caithness, tel. 01955 602596

➤ **Mountain Biking**
Forestry Enterprise, Highland Regional Office, 21 Church Street, Inverness, tel. 01463 232811, publishes a number of leaflets on mountain biking, some of which are free.

➤ **Special Events**
Caithness Highland Gathering takes place in Wick at the beginning of July, while Durness Highland Gathering takes place at the end of the month. Many other towns in the region have summer festivals and galas. Look out locally for more information.

GRAND TOUR

Route 24:
◆ Ullapool-Kylesku-Durness-Lairg-Inverness
◆
(◆) See Fact Sheets 20, 21 and 22

Stage 1: Ullapool-Kylesku

Ullapool, located on the northern shore of Loch Broom, is a bustling little town which has a slight frontier feel to it, especially in winter, when the Russian Klondyke fleet is anchored here. Ullapool was specifically developed as a fishing town by the British Fisheries Society in the 1780s, and is now the ferry port for Stornoway. The busiest place in Ullapool is the friendly Ceilidh Place, with its café, pub and live music. The Loch Broom Highland Museum is near the pier, and there are various nature cruises – try the *Summer Queen*, tel. 01854 612472.

Leave town on the A835, following the coast northwest. As the road turns to the right you can look down to Isle Martin, an RSPB reserve. About 6 miles out of Ullapool, going up Strath Kanaird, is a little bridge close to a hydroelectric power station. This is the start of the rough mountain bike route west to Achiltibuie (see Route 26).

The route carries on up Strath Kanaird, passing a junction signed to Achiltibuie, which is the start of Route 25 round the recommended Lochinver Peninsula. All the time there are views of the mountains of Coigach, Stac Polly and many others.

➤ 110

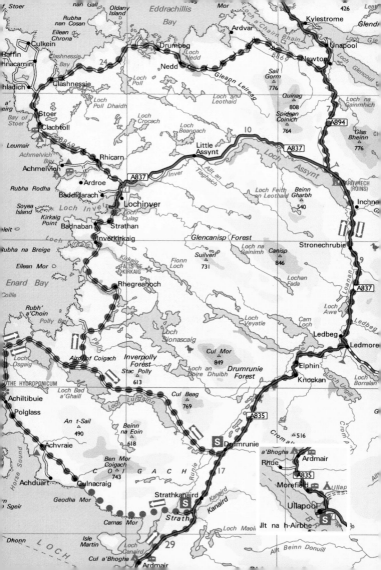

Ullapool & Lochinver

Fact Sheet 20 ●

The area from Coigach to Lochinver has the most magnificent scenery any-where in Scotland, and possibly in Europe. Looking at the contours on OS map 15 will give you some idea of how steep are some of the hills hereabouts. This is the land of short, sharp shocks going up and death-defying swoops back down again. It is tremendously rewarding, but you must be properly prepared. Carrying your own food is essential, and it can be a long way to the nearest bike repair shop. But if you do get this far north you should spend some time here and savour the unique atmosphere and the wonderful scenery.

➤ **OS Maps 15, 19, 20**

➤ **Tourist Information Offices (Summer only)**
Lochinver, Main Street, tel. 01571 844330
Ullapool, Argyle Street, tel. 01854 612135

➤ **Ferry**
Ullapool-Stornoway
Caledonian Macbrayne, tel. 01475 650100

➤ **Buses**
These will sometimes carry bikes at the driver's discretion. Rapson's, tel. 01463 710555, and Macdonald's, tel. 01851 706267, both operate to Ullapool, while Inverness Traction, Great Barnett Road, Inverness, tel. 01463 239292, oper-ates a service from Ullapool to Durness via Lochinver. For other bus services from Inverness, contact CityLink, tel. 0990 505050.

➤ **Cycle Shops**
Ullapool Mountain Bike Hire, 11 Pulteney Street, tel. 01854 612260
In an emergency ask at the Albannach House Hotel, Baddidarach, Lochinver, tel. 01571 844407, which has some bikes for hire, mainly for hotel residents.

➤ **Hostels**
SYHA, Ullapool, Shore Street, tel. 01854 612254
SYHA, Achmelvich, 4 miles north of Lochinver, tel. 01571 844480.
Near a beach with lots of lovely white sand.
SYHA, Achininver, 2.5 miles south of Achiltibuie, no telephone.
Ceilidh Place, Ullapool, tel. 01854 612103. Cheapish hotel with great food.
Live folk music.Separate bunkhouse with reasonable accommodation.
Tigh na Mara Vegetarian Guest House, Ardindrean, Loch Broom, tel. 01854 655282. Mountain bike hire.

➤ **Banks**
Royal Bank of Scotland, Ladysmith Street, Ullapool, tel. 01854 612112

➤ **Launderette**
Broomfield Caravan Site, West Lane, Ullapool, tel. 01854 612664

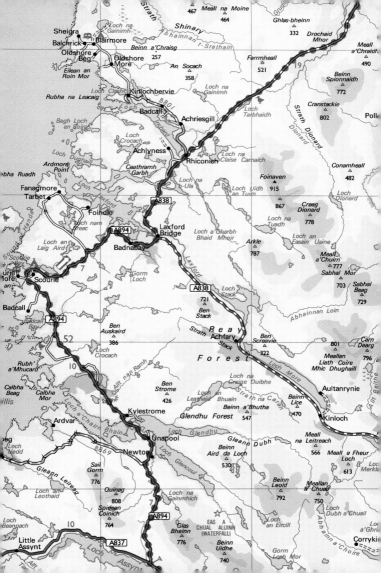

These hills are not particularly big but they are craggy and very impressive. Further on is the Knockan Visitor Centre, which is free and has details on the Inverpolly Nature Reserve west of here. There are various nature and geological walks. At Elphin is a farm for rare breeds, which also has a tearoom. (Admission charge.)

At Ledmore the route turns north on the A837, and there is an easy cycle to Inchnadamph, which has a hotel, and is a Mecca for geologists and cavers. The area is mainly limestone and evidence in the rock suggests that the caves were inhabited by Upper Palaeolithic man after the last Ice Age. Nearby is Ardvreck Castle, erstwhile seat of the Macleods, seized by the Mackenzies and now a ruin, jutting picturesquely into Loch Assynt. It seems a popular place for camping wild. Calda House is a burnt-out shell of another castle near Ardvreck.

At Skiag Bridge turn right on the A894 to Kylesku. This is a hilly road with great views of the exquisitely named Quinag, before dropping down to Kylesku for a well-deserved break. The pub here is friendly. From Kylesku you can take boat trips on Loch Glencoul, tel. 01571 844446, to Eas a' Chaul Aluinn, Britain's highest waterfall at 658 ft. There used to be a ferry across the loch before the bridge was built in the 1970s.

Stage 2: Kylesku-Durness

The craggy scenery around Laxford and Scourie is less overtly spectacular than some of the melodramatic peaks like Quinag and Coigach, yet the rock around Laxford is the oldest found in Europe and the landscape is positively lunar. This area is where veteran explorer and philosopher John Ridgeway operates his outdoor training courses for leaders of industry. He made his reputation rowing across the Atlantic with Chay Blyth.

Another interesting attraction is a native woodlands tree nursery just south of Scourie. It's incredible that trees grow so far north. Kinlochbervie is a worthwhile diversion along the B801 from Rhiconich, and makes a good overnight stop. It is a busy fishing port with a wonderful atmosphere, and also has a photogenic herd of Highland cattle. The hotel is friendly, though not cheap, and has good malt whiskies.

Continue north to Durness. Access to wild Cape Wrath is controlled by the army, which uses it as a weapons range, the only live ➤ 113

Fact Sheet 21 .... Caithness & Sutherland

Touring in the north of Scotland is a great experience – the sense of remoteness is complete, in summer the long, light evenings are a real plus, and the extraordinary landscape seems almost lunar in nature. Navigation is also extremely easy, as there are very few roads. In fact, if you are on a road, it's probably the right road! There are a fair number of pubs and other facilities, but this area is still very empty, so it's best to be self-sufficient. Some of the details given here are off the set route to give you more flexibility.

➤ OS Maps 9, 10, 16, 20, 21

➤ **Tourist Information Offices (Summer only)**
 Bettyhill, Clachan, Sutherland, tel. 01641 521342
 Durness, Sango, Sutherland, tel. 01971 511259
 Helmsdale, Coupar Park, Caithness, tel. 01431 821640
 Lairg, Sutherland, tel. 01549 402160
 Thurso, Riverside, Caithness, tel. 01847 892371

➤ **Ferry**
 Cromarty-Nigg
 Seaboard Marine, Tain, tel. 01862 871254

➤ **Cycle Shops**
 Pedal Power, Unit 1, Helmsdale Industrial Estate, Helmsdale,
 tel. 01431 821229
 Tain Cycles, Blairlaith Estate, Tain, tel. 01862 893332. 24 hr mobile repairs.
 Dryburgh Cycles, Tulloch Street, Dingwall, tel. 01349 862163
 Ken Ross Cycles, 2 Munro Street, Invergordon, tel. 01349 852538
 Leisure Activities, 11 Princes Street, Thurso, tel. 01847 895385
 Bike & Camping Shop, 354 High Street, Thurso, tel. 01847 896124
 Wheels, Glamis Road, Wick, tel. 01955 603636

➤ **Hostels**
 SYHA, Tongue, Sutherland, tel. 01847 611301
 SYHA, John o' Groats, Canisbay, Wick, Caithness, tel. 01955 611424
 SYHA, Helmsdale, Sutherland, tel. 01431 821577
 SYHA, Carbisdale Castle, Culrain, Sutherland, tel. 01549 421232
 Thurso Independent Hostel, Old Mill, Millbank, Thurso, Caithness,
 tel. 01847 892964
 Kylesku Lodges, Kylesku, Sutherland, tel. 01971 502003

➤ **Remote Hotels**
 Included due to the remoteness of the area. Details on B&Bs can be obtained
 from Tourist Information Offices.

Bettyhill Hotel, Bettyhill, Sutherland, tel. 01641 521352
Crask Inn, near Altnaharra, Sutherland, tel. 01520 744241
Altnaharra Hotel, at the south end of Loch Naver, Sutherland, tel. 01549 411222. Fairly pricey.
Kinlochbervie Hotel, Sutherland, tel. 01971 521275. 4 miles west of the A838 on the B801.
Rhiconich Hotel, tel. 01971 521224. 12 miles north of Scourie, Sutherland.
Kylesku Hotel, tel. 01971 502231. 10 miles south of Scourie, Sutherland. Boat trips go from the pier to Eas a' Chaul Aluinn, Britain's highest waterfall.
Ben Loyal Hotel, Tongue, Sutherland, tel. 01847 611216
Balintore Hostel, East Street, Balintore, Ross-shire, tel. 01862 832219

➤ **Banks**
These can be found in Lochinver, Thurso, Wick, Dingwall, Helmsdale, Tain and Invergordon.

➤ **Launderettes**
The Washtub, Riverside Place, Thurso, Caithness, tel. 01847 893266
Dunroamin Caravan Park, Helmsdale, Caithness, tel. 01549 402447

ammunition range in Britain. Boats leave from the Kyle of Durness to Cape Wrath (Mr Morrison, tel. 01971 511376), and the boat links with a seasonal (May-September) minibus (Mrs Mackay, tel. 01971 511343). The cliffs are a birdwatcher's paradise and the views and rock structures are spectacular.

At Balnakeil village, just outside Durness, there is a lovely beach. The former RAF camp is now a craft village and artists' colony. Boat trips go from Durness to nearby Smoo Caves, huge caverns cut into the cliffs. More details are available from the Tourist Information Office.

Stage 3: Durness-Lairg

From Durness head east on the A838 past Loch Eriboll, with a number of very attractive beaches, and on to the Kyle of Tongue, another beautiful sea loch. The loch is shallow and it is possible to walk out to Rabbit Island at low tide. Castle Varrish is a 14thC ruin which looks mean and moody. It is built on the site of a Norse stronghold. At this point you could head south on the more direct A836 to Lairg.

However, the full Grand Tour continues 10 miles further east to Strathnaver, a beautiful wooded valley. At the mouth of the River

Naver is a nature reserve, and close to it is Baile Marghait, once a Neolithic community. Strathnaver Museum near Bettyhill is housed in a converted church and has an account of the appalling Highland Clearances of 1814, when Patrick Sellars had thousands of people cleared from the glen and then set fire to their houses. Many died of hypothermia. The Countess of Sutherland followed his example and cleared many more people five years later. (Free.)

Altnaharra has a fishing hotel with comfortable sofas and good coffee. It's pricey, but dogs can be kept in your room for £1 extra! It is etched in my mind as the estate for which the landowner, Lord Kimball – a Tory peer – attempted to claim huge amounts of public money to protect Sites of Special Scientific Interest which would be affected by his forestry plans.

The next stage up Strath Vagastie leads to the Crask Inn, a classic drovers' inn with some accommodation, and it is something of a slog to get there. From here there is a roaring freewheel downhill towards Lairg and Bonar Bridge.

Stage 4: Lairg-Inverness

There's not much at Lairg apart from a railway station, but being situated at the south end of Loch Shin, it is popular with fishermen and hunters. In August the town hosts the largest sheep sales in Britain. Five miles beyond Lairg are the Falls of Shin, with a great coffee shop nearby.

Near Culrain is the amazing Carbisdale Castle, now a youth hostel, which was once owned by the Dukes of Sutherland. There are 'Highland Nights' in summer and the hostel also hires out bikes.

At Bonar Bridge the tradition of fishing with nets at the river mouth continues, though less than in the past. Owners of salmon rivers are keen to reduce the taking of fish in this way because it undermines the expensive fishing beats further upstream.

Follow the A836 along the south side of the Dornoch Firth and after about 4 miles take the B9176 signed to Alness. This is quite a climb but it gets you onto quiet roads and there is the Aultnamain Inn, another well-situated drovers' inn, at the top for refreshments. Take the first road left after the pub and take little roads towards Nigg. There is an independent hostel on the coast at Balintore.

Black Isle & Cromarty

Fact Sheet 22 . . . .

➤ **OS Map 21**

➤ **Tourist Information Office**
North Kessock (see Fact Sheet on page 105)

➤ **Ferry**
Nigg-Cromarty
Seaboard Marine, Tain, tel. 01862 871254

➤ **Cycle Shops**
See Fact Sheet 19

➤ **Hostels**
Cromarty Hotel, Cromarty, Ross-shire, tel. 01381 600217. Good food but changed hands recently.
Balintore Hostel, East Street, Balintore, Tain, Ross-shire, tel. 01862 832219

➤ **Banks**
Bank of Scotland, High Street, Cromarty, tel. 01381 600206

Cross the Cromarty Firth. Cromarty is a lovely historic town, with much to see. (Route 27 has more information about the Black Isle and Cromarty.) The route crosses farmland on fairly quiet roads and wends its way via Rosemarkie, the historic cathedral town of Fortrose, and Munlochy to North Kessock. The Kessock Bridge is not particularly cycle-friendly, but a pedestrian walkway can be used by cyclists. From here, take the busy A9, following signs for Inverness.

◆ Route 25: Achiltibuie & Lochinver
◆ **See Fact Sheet 20 and first Map for Route 24**

This route goes through one of the best cycling areas in Scotland, and starts about 10 miles north of Ullapool at Drumrunie, in the shadow of the gloomy bulk of Coigach. The route runs alongside

Loch Lurgainn and Loch Bad a'Ghaill, with Stac Polly on the right. This mountain is relatively small – 2009 ft – but makes a splendid viewpoint. It is well worth scrambling up, but appropriate equipment and considerable care are needed.

Continue to Achiltibuie and explore the south of the Lochinver Peninsula first. This is a quiet and beautiful area. The Summer Isles are wonderful and boat trips leave from Achiltibuie. The hotel is quite good and is owned by the family of Lucy Irvine, who became famous after answering Gerald Kingsland's advert to go with him to a desert island as a Girl Friday, and was the subject of the book and film called *Castaway*. Eventually backtrack to the Aird of Coigach and head north to Lochinver along a delightful little road. Be careful of tourist traffic. Lochinver is an attractive little town with pubs and lots of fishermen. The Lochinver Visitor Centre has displays on the people of the area as well as the magnificent surrounding landscape. (Free.) A short distance northwest in a lovely position is the Achmelvich hostel.

The final part of the route follows the B869 across the north of the peninsula via Drumbeg, where there is a hotel. This is a very hilly and spectacular route. Eventually the road joins the A894. Turn right via Ledmore to return to Drumrunie and Ullapool, and turn left to continue on Route 24 further north.

Route 26: Mountain Bike Route to Achiltibuie

See Fact Sheet 20 and first Map for Route 24

This route starts 7 miles north of Ullapool and involves 5 miles of rough footpath (see OS map) opposite Isle Martin and along the shore. This joins up with the road at Culnacraig, which continues to Achiltibuie. While the path is a bit of a struggle, involving some carrying, this is a satisfying route as it allows the complete circumnavigation of Coigach and has some wonderful views.

There are various interesting attractions at Achiltibuie, including the hydroponicum, which has a café and guided tours. This is a greenhouse-like structure in which plants are grown using aqua culture, a system which involves no soil. (Admission charge.) There is also a smokehouse. Achiltibuie is a great place for a holiday base. Past

Achiltibuie, continue along the coast past Polbain and up to Altandhu before turning east to the Aird of Coigach. Follow Route 25 in reverse back to Drumrunie on the A835.

Route 27: Cromarty Loop

See Fact Sheet 22 and last Map for Route 24

The route starts and ends at Cromarty, where there is plenty of parking. Cromarty was once a Royal Burgh and an important trading station. It produced much of the rope used in Nelson's fleet and also exported linen and iron. The merchants' houses reflect the town's glory days. Though it is now less prosperous than it was, the Kessock Bridge over the Beauly Firth from Inverness has rejuvenated the economy of the whole of the Black Isle. The current laird, Kent-based Sir Michael Nightingale, was in the national news recently, when he used his powers of feudal superiority to preempt the purchase of a house in his barony.

Hugh Miller's Cottage commemorates the life of Hugh Miller (1802-56), a remarkable figure of the Scottish Enlightenment. A geologist, naturalist, stonemason and theologian, he is perhaps best remembered for his radical pamphlets and other liberal writings. He also wrote about the Brahan Seer, who is said to have prophesied the Clearances. (Admission charge.)

Another popular attraction is the Dolphin Ecosse Tours, tel. 01381 600323, which leave from Cromarty pier. The bottle-nose dolphins grow up to 12 ft and regularly jump around the boat. Bill Fraser, the skipper, has signed up to a Dolphin Space Programme, a wildlife project aimed at safeguarding the welfare of the colony of 100 or so dolphins. However, he recently made film footage of the dolphins attacking and killing a porpoise in a way that challenges the widely held belief that they are friendly creatures.

The route takes the 'shore road', the B9163, along the south side of the Cromarty Firth to Jemimaville, before turning south signposted to Rosemarkie on the B9160 and the A832. Rosemarkie is an attractive village and in the Groam House Museum there are important Pictish stones and more information on the Brahan Seer. (Admission charge.) Retrace your route from the village and take an unclassified road on the right back towards Cromarty via Craighead and Navity. The whole of the route follows quiet country roads through rich farm-land and rolling hills, and there are many pleasant views of both the Cromarty Firth and Moray Firth, as well as inland.

The Forestry Commission has created several mountain bike routes through-out the north of Scotland. These are at Ardross near Tain; Lybster; Lael near Ullapool; the Black Isle; Achormlarie, near Loch Fleet south of Golspie; Torrachilty, near Strathpeffer; and Truderscraig and Borgie, near Strathnaver. These are all waymarked by the Forestry Commission, and leaflets and more details can be obtained from the Forest District Office, Dornoch, tel. 01862 810359, or the Forest District Office, Inverness, tel. 01463 791575.

SPEYSIDE & THE GRAMPIANS

Speyside and Scotland's East Coast are great places for cycling. The climate is far drier than the West Coast, and there are pretty towns, wonderful distilleries and lots of little back roads crying out to be explored. The Grand Tour over the eastern Cairngorms is hilly and the Cock Bridge to Tomintoul road is frequently closed in winter. Speyside Tourist Board organizes a Cyclist Welcome scheme, with a Speyside Cycle Trail and accommodation which includes cycle storage and washing facilities for people and bikes! Pick up the excellent leaflet at Tourist Information Offices.

➤ **Route 28 (Grand Tour)**
Inverness-Tomintoul-Crathie-Banchory
◆◆◆ Strenuous, with steep climb from Tomintoul over to Cock Bridge.
109 miles.

➤ **Route 29**
Dufftown-Glenlivet Loop
◆ (◆) Easy to moderate. 33 miles.

➤ **Route 30**
Tomintoul-Glenlivet Loop
◆ Easy. 19 miles.

➤ **Route 31**
Aviemore Circular
◆ Easy. 26 miles.

➤ **Route 32**
Forres & Elgin
◆◆ Moderate. 39 miles.

➤ **Route 33**
Glen Avon Mountain Bike Route
◆◆◆ Strenuous. 25 miles.

➤ **Rail**
The northeast of Scotland is served by the Aberdeen-Inverness route, with stations at, among other places, Elgin, Keith and Huntly. Tel. 0345 484950 (enquiries) or 0345 550033 (bookings).

➤ **Cycle Tour Organizers**
Roundabout Scotland, See page 227.

➤ **Tourist Information Offices (Open all year)**
Aberdeen, St Nicholas House, Broad Street, tel. 01224 632727

Aviemore, Grampian Road, tel. 01764 664235
Banchory, Bridge Street, tel. 01330 822000
Braemar, The Mews, Mar Road, tel. 01339 741600
Elgin, 17 High Street, tel. 01343 542666

➤ **Special Events**
The Malt Whisky Trail takes in eight Speyside distilleries – extreme care is
needed when cycling if you partake of a wee dram. A leaflet on the trail is
available at Tourist Information Offices. Dufftown Highland Games take place
in July, while September heralds the Aboyne Highland Gathering, and perhaps
the most famous Highland event, the Braemar Royal Highland Gathering.

GRAND TOUR

Route 28:

Inverness-Tomintoul-Crathie-Banchory

See Fact Sheets 23 and 24

Leave Inverness on the B9006 (see map on page 117), which climbs
through the suburb of Westhill and continues to Culloden battlefield.
Culloden is where Bonnie Prince Charlie's troops suffered a devastat-
ing defeat at the hands of the Duke of Cumberland's troops on 16
April 1746, and is now owned by the National Trust for Scotland,
whose visitor centre has audiovisual displays and is housed in the
heather-thatched Old Leanach Cottage. (Admission charge.) A cere-
mony is held every year to commemorate the carnage of the battle.

Continue west on the B9006 for 6 miles to a junction with the B9090.
Turn right for Cawdor, which is worth visiting for its Shakespearean
connection. Macbeth becomes Thane of Cawdor and part of the
witches' prophecy comes true. The castle dates from 1372 and has
massive towers, a drawbridge, gardens, a putting green and nature
trails. (Admission charge.)

Take the unclassified road west to join the A939 near Redburn. At
Ferness is Ardclach Bell Tower. It dates back to 1655 and is a small
fairy-tale house. It served as a prison and watchtower, as well as sum-
moning the parishioners to the nearby and now-deserted ➤ 127

Fact Sheet 23 . . . .

Speyside

This is a wonderful area for cycling. It is quite well served by facilities such as teashops and tourist attractions, as this is also a popular area for visitors. However, it is not as much of a scrum as Loch Ness. This is Scotland's 'Big Country', with graceful rivers and beautiful heather-covered hills, particularly impressive in August and September.

➤ OS Maps 26, 27, 36, 37

➤ **Tourist Information Offices (Summer only)**
Dufftown, The Clock Tower, The Square, tel. 01340 820501
Grantown-on-Spey, High Street, tel. 01479 872773
Tomintoul, The Square, tel. 01807 580285

➤ **Cycle Shops**
Sports Hire, Grantown Road, Nethybridge, tel. 01479 821333. Spares and repairs.
Mini-cheers, 5 Fife Street, Dufftown, tel. 01340 820559. Repairs.
The Clockhouse Restaurant, The Square, Tomintoul, tel. 01807 580474. Repairs and bike hire.
ReCycles, Rafford, Forres, tel. 01309 672811
A. Junner, South Street, Elgin, tel. 01343 546412

➤ **Hostels**
SYHA, Tomintoul, Main Street, Ballindalloch. No telephone.
Jenny's Bothy, Dellachuper, Corgarff, Strathdon, Banffshire, tel. 01975 651446/9

➤ **Banks**
These can be found in Elgin, Forres and Grantown.

➤ **Launderettes**
The Cyclists Welcome Scheme includes accommodation with washing facilities and drying rooms. See leaflets available in Tourist Information Offices for more details.

➤ **Mountain Biking**
The Glenlivet estate around Tomintoul has various mountain bike trails, and publishes an excellent leaflet, tel. 01807 580283. Forestry Enterprise Fochabers, tel. 01343 820223, operates waymarked tracks and also publishes an explanatory leaflet.

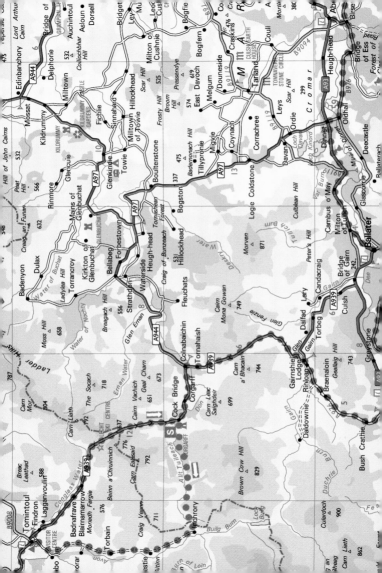

kirk, which was built in a valley and the sound of whose bells did not carry. Get the key at the roadside and put it back afterwards in its little glass box. Continue south on the A939 to Grantown-on-Spey. This town was an 18thC planned village and is rather nice, if slightly snobbish. It is a popular base for walking and skiing holidays around nearby Aviemore, and also for cycling.

The route to Tomintoul involves some hilly sections past Bridge of Brown and Bridge of Avon. There is pleasant moorland with some good views. The rivers in this area are also very pleasant for picnicking next to. Tomintoul is thought to be the highest village (1150 ft) in the Highlands. It becomes notorious in winter when the Tomintoul to Cock Bridge road is often blocked with snow. There is a ski area at Lecht with a tearoom. The route here climbs to a knee-cracking 2116 ft.

At Cock Bridge are the gloomy ruins of Corgarff Castle, and an independent hostel. The castle was built about 1550, burned down and rebuilt. After 1746 it was once again rebuilt as a Hanoverian barracks. (Admission charge.) The route continues south on the A939 for 6 miles to a junction with the B976. Follow signs to Crathie.

Crathie Kirk is an unpretentious little church used occasionally by the royal family when they stay at nearby Balmoral. It was built for and opened by Queen Victoria in 1895. The River Dee runs picturesquely by and it is fun to watch photographers stalking the riverbank hoping for pictures of stray royals. Balmoral Castle and grounds are open to the public in May, June and July. Balmoral estate was bought in 1853 by Queen Victoria for £31,500. The castle is a fine, if rather overblown, example of Scots Baronial architecture. (Admission charge.) Note also the Royal Lochnagar Distillery, which dates from 1845. It has tours and a coffee shop. (Admission charge.)

Cross the river and take the delightful little road on the south bank of the Dee. Looking at the pleasant scenery gives you a good idea of why Queen Victoria decided to buy here. The route to Ballater is gently downhill. Ballater was built on a grid pattern in the late 18thC, to accommodate visitors attracted to the nearby spa of Pannanich Wells. The coming of the Deeside Railway to Ballater in 1867 increased the town's popularity.

Further down river is Cambus o' May Suspension Bridge, built in 1905 to the same design as the earlier one at Pollhollock. As it was in poor repair it was replaced in the 1980s by Kincardine and Deeside

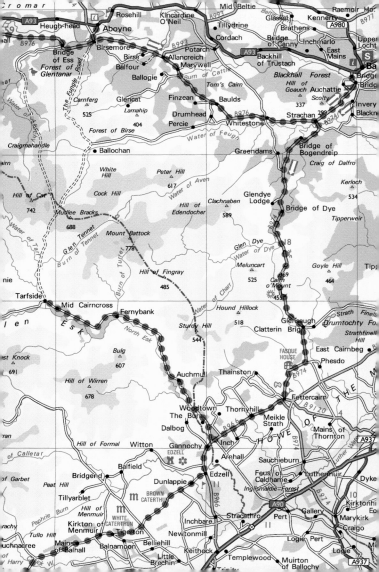

Council and opened in 1988 by the Queen Mother. Cross the river at Dinnet and follow the B976 and B974. Aboyne and Banchory are both pleasant towns with plenty of services.

Fact Sheet 24 • **Royal Deeside**

Royal Deeside, a peaceful glen with wonderful trees and scenery, comes with the seal of approval of Queen Victoria, who bought the Balmoral estate back in the middle of the last century. There are several mountain biking routes in the area, including some on the Balmoral estate itself.

➤ **Tourist Information Offices (Summer only)**
Aboyne, Ballater Road Car Park, tel. 01339 886060
Ballater, Station Square, tel. 01339 755306
Crathie, Car Park, Balmoral Castle, tel. 01339 742414

➤ **Cycle Shops**
Braemar Outdoor Centre, 15 Mar Road, tel. 01339 741442
Making Treks, Station Road, Ballater, tel. 01339 755865
Monster Bikes, Unit 2, North Deeside Road, Banchory, tel. 01330 825313
BG Cycles, The Barn, Aboyne, tel. 01339 885355

➤ **Hostels**
SYHA, Ballater, Deebank Road, tel. 01339 755227
SYHA, Braemar, Corrie Feragie, 21 Glenshee, tel. 01339 741659
Wolf Hearth, The Steading, Tornaveen, by Banchory, tel. 01339 883460
Braemar Bunkhouse, Mar Road, Braemar, tel. 01339 741242
Jenny's Bothy, Dellachuper, Corgarff, Strathdon, tel. 01975 651446/9

➤ **Banks**
These can be found in Braemar, Ballater, Aboyne and Banchory.

➤ **Launderette**
Station Square, Aboyne, tel. 01339 786818/783458

➤ **Mountain Biking**
Forestry Enterprise, tel. 01330 844537, has a leaflet on trails round Banchory, while information on mountain bike routes around Braemar and Ballater can be obtained from local cycle shops.

Route 29: Dufftown-Glenlivet Loop

See Fact Sheet 23 and first Map for Route 28

Dufftown is a bustling little town at the centre of the malt whisky trail. This tour includes visits to various distilleries, but don't drink too much of the product – drinking and cycling is illegal. There are seven distilleries built around the town between 1823 and 1898, and they are a big tourist attraction. Other attractions are the ancient Mortlach Kirk, with interesting Pictish stones in the vestibule, and Balvenie Castle, in a romantic setting between the rivers Fiddoch and Rinnes, once owned by the Black Douglases and visited in 1562 by Mary Queen of Scots. It is now a ruin. (Admission charge.)

Dufftown even has its own ditty:

Rome was built on seven hills,
Dufftown stands on seven stills.

Dufftown is the home of Glenfiddich, which claims to be 'Chateau Bottled'. The distillery has a visitor centre, tel. 01340 820373. (Free.) It was established by William Grant in 1886 with the able assistance of his seven sons. It is a great commercial success and the whisky isn't bad either! The Grant family control many of the distilleries in this area. From Dufftown take the B9009 southwest up Glen Rinnes about 10 miles to Auchbreck, then turn right on the B9008 to Glenlivet and the Glenlivet Distillery, tel. 01542 783220, complete with a coffee shop. (Free.)

From Glenlivet turn north on the B9008, following the River Avon. At Bridge of Avon you pass the Delnashaugh Inn. The river here is famous for its salmon. Near the River Spey is Ballindalloch Castle, owned by the Grant family. Turn right on the A95 for 2 miles to the Glenfarclas Distillery. This is another Grant family distillery, tel. 01807 500245. (Admission charge.)

Take the B9138 over the Spey then turn right on the Speyside Way. The route is rather pleasant and passes Knockando, where the Cardhu Distillery has a coffee shop, tel. 01340 810204. Continue down the Spey, following the signposts to Charlestown of Aberlour and Craigellachie, where you can watch craftsmen in Britain's only remaining working cooperage, tel. 01340 871108. (Admission charge.)

Follow the Speyside Way along the River Fiddich back to Dufftown.

MALT WHISKY

Malt whisky is produced using only three ingredients: barley, Highland water and yeast. This is the procedure:

Malting. Barley is steeped in water then allowed to germinate until roots and shoots start to appear. During germination, enzymes are produced which can convert the starch in the barley to fermentable sugars. Germination is then stopped by drying the grain, or 'green malt' as it is known, in the malt kiln over a peat fire whose smoke helps give whisky its peaty taste.

Mashing. The malt is milled and the ground malt or 'grist' is mashed or mixed with hot water and fed into a mash tun. The soluble starch is thus converted into a sugary liquid known as wort, which is drawn off from the mash for fermentation.

Fermentation. After cooling the wort is passed into large copper vessels known as washbacks, where it is fermented by yeast into a weak alcoholic solution.

Distillation. The wash is distilled twice in large copper pot stills. The first distillation in the wash still produces a liquid called low wines which is distilled again in the low wines still to produce spirit. At this stage it is the stillman who contributes to the traditional quality and flavour of his distillery's malt whisky. Only the middle portion of the second distillation is collected.

Maturation. The newly distilled spirit is put in oak casks and transferred to a warehouse where it is left to mature for a number of years. During maturation the spirit loses its sharpness, taking on the mellow mature flavour of the full-bodied single malt.

Bottling. After maturation the whisky is reduced to the strength required by the addition of soft water. The whisky is then filtered carefully and put in bottles which are sealed and labelled. The bottles are then packed in cases and sent off.

Route 30: Tomintoul-Glenlivet Loop

See Fact Sheet 23 and first Map for Route 28

Tomintoul is thought to be the highest village in the Highlands, and is surrounded by moorland. There is a museum in The Square about rural life, tel. 01309 673701. (Free.) There is also a small youth hostel (no phone). The route heads north on the B9008 to Glenlivet, where you should visit the fascinating distillery, which also has a coffee shop, tel. 01542 783220. (Free.)

Return to Tomintoul on the B9136 via Strath Avon, which is very scenic. Turn left after about 10 miles and take the unclassified road signed to Tomintoul. The Speyside Way also runs cross-country between Tomintoul and Glenlivet, and is a rough alternative route suitable for mountain bikes.

Route 31: Aviemore Circular

See Fact Sheet 25

Aviemore was radically redeveloped in the 1960s as a purpose-built resort for skiing. The town is rather ugly (though there are plans for major improvements), but the Spey Valley in which it is situated is wonderful, with Caledonian pine woods and the surrounding Cairngorm Mountains. Visitors can take a chairlift up Cairn Gorm itself, even in summer – a popular attraction. However, this is not without its problems as the high mountain plateau is a fragile ecosystem, and plans currently under consideration to build a funicular railway up the mountain have sharpened these concerns.

There are a fair number of mountain bike routes in this area, particularly in the Rothiemurchus and Abernethy forests. Ask at local bike shops for access details, or devise your own routes using OS maps 35, 36 and 43.

This route leaves Aviemore and heads east on the road signposted to the ski lifts. After a mile turn right onto the B970, following signs to Kincraig. The Inshriach Alpine Nursery was started by plantsman Jack

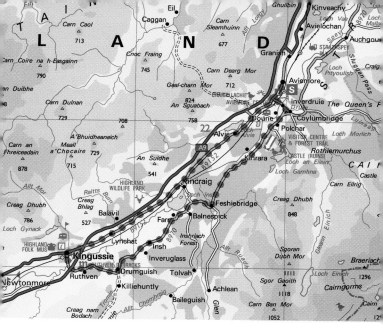

Drake. Further along is the Loch an Eilein Pottery, with its own shop. On Thursday they have a Throw-your-own-Pot Day, tel. 01479 810837. Further on, the Loch an Eilein Visitor Centre has a tearoom.

The road follows the course of the River Spey, crosses the River Feshie and continues past Loch Insh, a recommended tea stop. The watersports centre here is run by one Clive Freshwater. Continue on the B970 and just before Kingussie are the Ruthven Barracks, built in 1718 as a base from which to suppress Jacobite uprisings, and blown up by Bonnie Prince Charlie's forces after Culloden. (Free.) In Kingussie is the Highland Folk Museum, tel. 01540 661307, housed partly in a shooting lodge and partly outdoors. It has a black house, clack (grain) mill and farming artefacts, and also has displays on other aspects of Highland life, including music.

From Kingussie, which has various cafés and restaurants, return on the west side of the Spey to Aviemore on the B9152. Make sure you avoid the very busy A9. After a mile is a monument to local man

James Macpherson, an 18thC poet who claimed to have rediscovered and translated poems by Ossian, son of Fingal. The work was published in 1773 and became a sensation, though it was greeted with scepticism by Samuel Johnson, who thought it was literary fraud. A committee of the Highland Society of Scotland investigated whether or not the Ossianic poems existed, with inconclusive results. Whatever, the poems still have a widespread appeal, both for their romanticism and for their 'noble savage' view of the Highlander. Continue northeast on the B9152 back to Aviemore.

Fact Sheet 25 · · · · · · · · · · · · **Aviemore & Kingussie**

The Spey Valley is one of the most popular tourist areas in Scotland. There are beautiful forests and Britain's most extensive mountain range, plus steam trains and a variety of museums and other visitor attractions. However, if you want solitude this is probably not the best place to be.

➤ **OS Maps 35, 36**

➤ **Tourist Information Offices (Summer only)**
Carrbridge, Main Street, tel. 01479 841630
Kingussie, King Street, tel. 01540 661297

➤ **Cycle Shops**
Speyside Sports, Main Road, Aviemore, tel. 01479 810656
Inverdruie Mountain Bikes, Rochiemurchus Visitor Centre, near Aviemore, tel. 01479 810787
Loch Insh Watersports Centre, Loch Insh, Kincraig, tel. 01540 651272.
Bike hire, and also a teashop.

➤ **Hostels**
SYHA, Aviemore, 25 Grampian Road, tel. 01479 810345
SYHA, Loch Morlich, Glenmore, tel. 01479 861238
SYHA, Glen Feshie, Balachoick, Glen Feshie, tel. 01540 601323
Kirkbeag Cabin, Kincraig, Kingussie, tel. 01540 651298

➤ **Banks**
There are branches in Aviemore and Kingussie.

➤ **Launderette**
At Aviemore hostel (see above).

Route 32: Forres & Elgin

See Fact Sheet 26

Forres is a lovely little town which frequently wins the Britain in Bloom Competition and is near where Macbeth and Banquo met the witches on a blasted heath in Shakespeare's play. The Falconer Museum, tel. 01309 673701, has exhibits on local, social and natural history, and also has a display about the folk singers The Corries. (Free.) Sueno's Stone is a remarkable Pictish stone, 20 ft high and dating from the 9th or 10thC. It is elaborately carved with a battle scene. The town has a Highland Games in July.

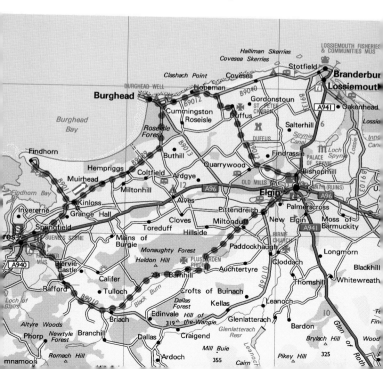

Forres & Elgin

Fact Sheet 26 ....

This area is very fertile and enjoys a (statistically) warmer and drier climate than the West Coast. It is a prosperous farming area with lots of back roads to explore. There are also many unusual places to visit, and a number of attractive towns.

➤ **OS Maps, 27, 28**

➤ **Tourist Information Office (Summer only)**
  Forres, 116 High Street, tel. 01309 672938

➤ **Cycle Shops**
  Junner, South Street, Elgin, tel. 01343 540559
  ReCycles, Rafford, Forres, tel. 01309 672811
  Stuarts of Forres, 32 High Street, Forres, tel. 01309 672432

➤ **Hostel**
  Saltire Lodge, Pluscarden Road, Elgin, tel. 01343 550624

➤ **Banks**
  These can be found in Elgin and Forres.

Leave Forres on the B9011. At Kinloss the B9011 leads to the coastal village of Findhorn, home to the New-Age Findhorn Foundation, tel. 01309 691258, which has a substantial alternative lifestyle community developing ecological housing and the Trees for Life Project. There is also a nice friendly café. Return to Kinloss and continue to Burghead, with its small port. The village still has a fishing tradition, although most boats are now kept in Fraserburgh or Peterhead. The promontory is the site of a Pictish fort, though little remains. Some Pictish carvings are housed in Burghead Museum. There is also a well, with a walkway which is sometimes open. It is known as the Roman Well but in fact it is thought to be Pictish or early Christian. In January Burghead 'Burns the Clavie', when a burning barrel is carried through the streets, continuing the tradition of a pagan fire ritual.

Continue on the B9012, swinging south through Duffus and on towards Elgin. Duffus Castle, a ruined motte and bailey which still has its moat intact and full of water, has a 14thC tower and was the original seat of the Murrays, who renamed themselves the De Moravias. They later became the Dukes of Atholl and Sutherland.

Elgin is an attractive market town with a particularly lovely ruined Cathedral (admission charge), known as 'The Lantern of the North', which dates from 1224 and was burnt down by the Wolf of Badenoch (see below). The cathedral was stripped of lead by the Privy Council and in 1650 Cromwell's troops smashed up more of it. However, it is still very fine, and a 6thC Pictish slab remains in the choir. It is also worth visiting Elgin Museum, tel. 01343 543675, in High Street, which has a world-famous collection of fossils. (Admission charge.)

From Elgin take the B9010 south and turn right after 1.5 miles on an unclassified road though Miltonduff to Pluscarden Abbey. The abbey is run by Benedictine monks and dates from 1230, but was wrecked by the Wolf of Badenoch. It was taken over by Benedictines in 1454 but changed hands, before passing back to the Order in 1943. The monks still wear white habits and you are welcome to visit any time.

Continue to the B9010. Return via Rafford to Forres.

WOLF OF BADENOCH

The Wolf of Badenoch was the nickname of Alexander Stewart, Earl of Buchan (1343-1405), the violent natural son of Robert II who had lands in Badenoch around Kingussie. He was excommunicated by the Bishop of Moray for leaving his lawful wife, the Countess of Ross, for another woman. In revenge he destroyed Elgin and its cathedral, though he later did penance at the Mercat Cross for his atrocious deeds. An armoured effigy in Dunkeld Cathedral may be of him. In part his reputation is as a result of Sir Thomas Dick Lauder, who wrote a novel about him in 1870.

Route 33: Glen Avon Mountain Bike Route

See Fact Sheet 23 and second Map for Route 28

Start at either Cock Bridge or Tomintoul, where there are car parks. From Cock Bridge go up past Corgarff and take the track west along the River Don to Inchrory. Then take the rough track down Glen Avon to Tomintoul. From Tomintoul, take the steep old military road, now the A939, built by Hanoverian troops after Culloden, then screech back down into Corgarff.

Fact Sheet 27

Aberdeen

Aberdeen is a refreshingly no-nonsense city compared with the slightly snobbish Royal Deeside. It has a busy port, and ferries leave here for Orkney and Shetland. The oil boom has brought prosperity, with interesting restaurants and shops. Aberdeen is ideal for a rest stop while on a longer tour.

➤ **OS Map 38**

➤ **Tourist Information Office (Open all year)**
St Nicholas House, Broad Street, tel. 01224 632727

➤ **Rail**
Aberdeen is served by InterCity trains from London King's Cross, as well as from the Scottish Central Belt. Trains also operate to Inverness via Elgin. Tel. 0345 484950 (enquiries) or 0345 550033 (bookings).

➤ **Ferry**
Aberdeen-Lerwick, Shetland.
P&O, PO Box 5, Jamieson's Quay, Aberdeen, tel. 01224 572615

➤ **Cycle Shops**
Aberdeen Bothy Bikes, 120 John Street, tel. 01224 622544. Repairs, bike hire and some guided cycle tours.
Alpine Bikes, 66-70 Holburn Street, tel. 01224 211255
Cycling World, 460 George Street, tel. 01224 632994
Neill Ross, 232 King Street, tel. 01224 626360. Mountain bike specialist.

➤ **Hostels**
SYHA, Aberdeen, 8 Queen's Road, tel. 01224 646988

➤ **Launderettes**
Aberdeen Cleaning, 144 Crown Street, tel. 01224 590076

ANGUS & FIFE

• •

The glens of Angus and Fife have farm roads and wonderful forests, and are flanked by rolling hills. There are many interesting castles and historic remains. Fife is famed for its golf courses and picturesque fishing villages, and is another area of Scotland missed by many visitors. The area is relatively accessible by public transport and the cycling is fantastic.

➤ **Route 34 (Grand Tour)**
Banchory-Edzell-Dundee-Edinburgh
♦♦ Moderate, with some steep sections. 165 miles.

➤ **Route 35**
Glen Clova Loop
♦♦ Moderate. 38 miles.

➤ **Route 36**
Green Dundee Loop
♦ Easy.

➤ **Route 37**
East Fife Loop
♦ Easy. 23 miles.

➤ **Rail**
The main stations in the area are at Aberdeen, Perth and Dundee, all of which are served by trains from the Scottish Central Belt and also from England. There is also a minor railway route through Fife, including stations at Glenrothes, Kirkcaldy and Inverkeithing. All trains to Edinburgh cross the magnificent Forth Rail Bridge. Tel. 0345 484950 (enquiries) or 0345 550033 (bookings).

➤ **Cycle Tour Organizers**
Mountains and Glens, Railway Road, Blairgowrie, tel. 01250 874206. Bike hire and tours.
Scottish Cycling Holidays, Ballintruim Post Office, Blairgowrie, tel. 01250 886201. Bike hire and tours.

➤ **Tourist Information Offices (Open all year)**
Arbroath, Market Place, tel. 01241 872609
Banchory, Bridge Street, tel. 01330 822000
Blairgowrie, 26 Wellmeadow, tel. 01250 872960/873701
Dundee, 4 City Square, tel. 01382 434664
Dunfermline, 13/15 Maygate, tel. 01383 720999
Glenrothes, Kingdom Centre, Rothes Square, tel. 01592 754954

CHAPTER 8

Kinross, Service Area, off Junction 6, M90, tel. 01577 863680
Perth, 45 High Street, tel. 01738 638353
St Andrews, 70 Market Street, tel. 01334 472021

➤ **Special Events**
Dundee holds its summer festival in July and the Kirriemuir Music Festival
takes place in September.

GRAND TOUR
◆ Route 34: Banchory-Edzell-Dundee-Edinburgh
◆ See Fact Sheets 28 and 29

Stage 1: Banchory-Edzell

The Grand Tour continues south of Deeside from Banchory (see map
on page 128) and Strachan, and climbs on the B974 up Glen Dye
through pine forests to the heather-covered moor. The summit, Cairn
o' Mount, is 1488 ft above sea level. The B974 is an old military road,
part of the system built by the Hanoverian General Wade. The tree-
planting in Glen Dye was highly controversial in the late 1980s as
increasingly rare moorland habitats were sacrificed for commercial
cultivation. The moorland is a valuable hunting ground for a range of
birds of prey, including owls, golden eagles and peregrine falcons.
There are wonderful views.

Just before Fettercairn is Fasque House, tel. 01561 340569, a grand
Victorian pile bought in 1829 by Sir John Gladstone, father of the
famous prime minister who served four terms during Queen
Victoria's reign. Six generations later the Gladstone family are still
here. There is a magnificent cantilever staircase leading to the state-
rooms upstairs. (Admission charge.)

At Fettercairn an arch commemorates Queen Victoria's visit of 1861.
The Fettercairn Distillery, tel. 01561 340205, which does free tours, is
one of Scotland's oldest. It is known to have been operating in 1824
and is now owned by Whyte and Mackay.

The route goes southwest to Edzell, passing the entrance to Glen
Esk on the way. The B966 crosses the Gannochy Bridge, where you

Angus & Dundee

Fact Sheet 28 . . . .

The Angus glens roll down from the Grampian Mountains, and have fertile farmland. Around Kirriemuir is Scotland's main area for soft fruit growing. There is good cycling, with lots to see in terms of attractive towns, tourist sites and historic castles. Some of the roads can be busy and fast so care is required.

➤ OS Maps 44, 45, 54

➤ **Tourist Information Offices (Summer only)**
Brechin, St Ninian's Place, tel. 01356 623050
Carnoustie, High Street, tel. 01241 852258
Forfar, 40 East High Street, tel. 01307 467876
Kirriemuir, Cumberland Close, tel. 01575 574097

➤ **Cycle Shops**
Brewster Cycles, 120 Logie Street, Dundee, tel. 01382 669611
Bill Ramsay Bike Repair, 52 Main Street, Dairsle, Fife, tel. 01334 870890. Mobile repairs.
Just Bikes, 57 Gray Street, Broughty Ferry, Dundee, tel. 01382 732100
Woolers, 147 High Street, Lochee, Fife, tel. 01382 611628
Nicholson's Cycling Centre, 2 Forfar Road, Dundee, tel. 01382 461212
Mountain and Glens, Railway Road, Blairgowrie, tel. 01250 874206

➤ **Hostel**
SYHA, Glendoll, Glen Clova, north of Kirriemuir, tel. 01575 550236

➤ **Banks**
All the major Scottish banks are well represented in Dundee and there are branches in all the main towns in the region, including Arbroath, Brechin, Blairgowrie and Kirriemuir.

➤ **Launderettes**
Charleston Launderette, 87 Charleston Street, Dundee, tel. 01382 841932
Perth Road Launderette, 272 Perth Road, Dundee, tel. 01382 646906

can pass through a door in the wall to see the river which is full of rock pools, known as the Rocks of Solitude. You can see frequently salmon jumping upriver to spawn.

Edzell Castle, tel. 01356 648631, is where Mary Queen of Scots stayed in 1562. It is a splendid 16thC ruin with the even more impressive walled Pleasance gardens, which are very formal. The gardens

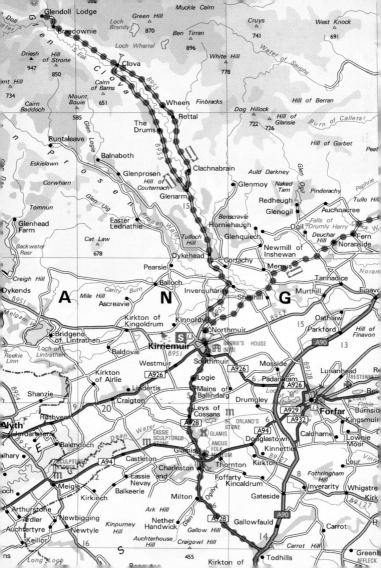

have relief sculpture panels with figures copied from prints by German Renaissance artist Dürer. (Admission charge.)

A diversion to Tarfside, 10 miles north, leads to the Glenesk Folk Museum, which is worth a visit if you have the time. It details the social history of the area from 1800. (Admission charge.)

Stage 2: Edzell-Dundee

Turn right just south of Edzell and take small farm roads west, following signs for Kirkton and Fern. A couple of miles takes you past the two Iron-Age forts of Brown and White Caterthun. Brown Caterthun has four concentric ramparts and ditches, and White Caterthun is in particularly good condition. The central stone fort is Brobdingnagian, with double walls.

The route rolls pleasantly, if uneventfully, along to the attractive town of Kirriemuir, birthplace in 1860 of J.M. Barrie, author of *Peter Pan*. Owned by the National Trust, it has a tearoom and exhibitions about Barrie's life and writing. Barrie was one of the kailyard school of writers – sentimental, romantic and slightly 'small town'. (Admission charge.) See also the Camera Obscura above the town, which gives panoramic views of the area. (Admission charge.) Vissochi's Café has wonderful traditional Italian ice cream – just like mamma used to make.

Head south on the A928 towards Glamis. Pronounced 'Glarms' – preferably in clipped 1940s English – this is the birthplace of Queen Elizabeth, the Queen Mother and Princess Margaret. The castle has links with Shakespeare's Macbeth – he was the Thane of Glamis – but today's many-turreted building only dates back to the 15thC and has had many additions since. There is a tearoom. (Admission charge.) You can see how the other, more down-to-earth, half lived at the Angus Folk Museum, a collection of agricultural cottages, nearby. (Admission charge.)

Other nearby historic sites are the Glamis Stone in the garden of the manse, by tradition the burial place of Malcolm II in 1034, though in fact the stone is older, and Eassie Sculptured Stone, west of Glamis in Eassie Churchyard, an elaborate carved standing stone.

The route continues on the A928. At Petterden cross the busy A90 dual carriageway, before cutting off onto back roads leading to the east end of Dundee, where the route links with Route 36.

Dundee is not the quaintest of Scottish cities but the patriot William Wallace, of *Braveheart* fame, went to school here. Dundee was built during a boom in whaling, and now is known for its jute, jam and journalism. It is home of D.C. Thomson, publishers of the *Beano*, the *Sunday Post* and *The People's Friend*, among others. It was from Dundee that the explorer Captain Scott set sail for Antarctica in 1901 in his ship *Discovery*, which has been restored as a tourist attraction. It is moored at Discovery Point, tel. 01382 201245. (Admission charge.) Nearby in Victoria Dock the frigate *Unicorn* is the oldest British ship afloat – it was launched in 1824. On a nice day it is worth climbing up the Law, north of the city, which has good views over Dundee and across the Tay estuary.

Stage 3: Dundee-Edinburgh

The route goes south from Dundee over the Tay Road Bridge. From here you can see the rail bridge. Naturally, this is not the bridge over the 'Silvery Tay', immortalized by William McGonagall, Scotland's – perhaps the world's – worst poet, which fell down with the loss of 75 lives in a terrible storm in 1879. McGonagall recorded ninety deaths. Is this poetic licence? The second bridge was built in 1887, on almost the same site as the first. A snatch of McGonagall's very long poem includes:

> So the train mov'd slowly along the Bridge of Tay
> Until it was about midway,
> Then the central girders with a crash gave way,
> And down went the train and the passengers into the Tay!
> The storm fiend did loudly bray,
> Because ninety lives had been taken away,
> On the last Sabbath day of 1879,
> Which will be remember'd for a very long time.

Once off the bridge, the route branches east to Leuchars via the B946 to Tayport, then the B945. OS Map 59 shows you can follow the coast round, taking in attractive Tentsmuir Sands, where seals loll around in the water. Sometimes even foolhardy Scots swim here! Leuchars is on the railway and has an RAF base. You should visit the splendid 16thC Earlshall Castle, still inhabited by the Baron of Earlshall. It was restored in the 1890s by the architect Sir Robert Lorimer, and has fascinating ceiling murals. Tel. 01334 839205. Tearoom. (Admission charge.)

From Leuchars the route heads towards St Andrews on the A919, then east for 0.25 mile on the busy A91, before branching off south to Strathkinness and into St Andrews on the B939. This takes you past the Botanic Gardens which have nice glasshouses, tel. 01334 477178.

Fact Sheet 29 .... **Fife & Perth**

The East Neuk of Fife is very attractive, and St Andrews is a great town, famous for its golf courses and ancient university. It also has nice beaches and there are tearooms everywhere! The little fishing villages round the coast are lovely. As you head further west the townscape becomes more industrial and less picturesque, and the traffic gets heavier. It is possible to avoid the unrewarding ride through east Fife to Edinburgh by catching trains from Kirkcaldy, Cupar or Glenrothes. There is a whole maze of little country roads through Fife and Perthshire which are great to explore, hell to find and even worse to describe. However, try to keep off the A9, A92, A85 and other main routes. The OS map for the area is invaluable.

➤ **OS Maps 58, 59**

➤ **Tourist Information Offices (Summer only)**
   Anstruther, Scottish Fisheries Museum, tel. 01333 310628
   Cupar, The Granary, Coal Road, tel. 01334 652874
   Forth Road Bridge, by North Queensferry, tel. 01383 417759

➤ **Cycle Shops**
   Leuchars Cycles, 2 Meadow Road, Leuchars, tel. 01577 838989
   Spokes, 77 South Street, St Andrews, tel. 01334 477835
   Stewarts, 31 Ladywynd, Cupar, tel. 01334 652202
   Bike World, 3 Ferguson Square, Cupar, tel. 01334 656339
   Richards, 44 George Street, Perth, tel. 01738 626860

➤ **Hostels**
   SYHA, Perth, Glasgow Road, tel. 01738 623658
   SYHA, Falkland, Back Wynd, tel. 01337 957710
   SYHA, Glendevon, Dollar, tel. 01259 781206
   SYHA, Stirling, Castle Wynd, tel. 01786 473442
   The Bunkhouse, West Pitkierie, near Anstruther, tel. 01333 310768

➤ **Banks**
   There are main branches in St Andrews, Dunfermline and Perth, as well as in other towns in the area.

➤ **Launderettes**
   Woodburn Terrace, St Andrews, tel. 01334 475150

St Andrews is famous as the home of golf and is popular with people wearing colourful sweaters. If you share their baffling interest in this game, visit the British Golf Museum, tel. 01334 478880, and relive its 500-year history. (Admission charge.) Of more general interest are the beautiful and ancient University, and the Museum of St Andrews in turreted Kinburn House which details the social history of the town, and also has a tearoom. (Free.) Children particularly like the Sea Life Centre, tel. 01334 474786, down by the harbour. (Admission charge.) St Andrews University was founded in 1412, and is one of the oldest in Britain. The red gowns worn by students on ceremonial occasions reputedly were introduced so they could be easily spotted entering brothels!

St Andrews has various other fine buildings, including the ruined Cathedral, and St Andrews Castle, built as a bishop's palace and notable for its horrific 14thC bottle dungeon, in which radical Protestants were thrown. Also, George Wishart, friend of John Knox, was burned at the stake here, while the sadistic Cardinal Beaton looked on. The Cathedral has a museum and splendid panoramic views. (Admission charges for cathedral and castle.)

From St Andrews head southeast on the A917, signposted to Crail. This eastern 'beak' of Fife is known as the East Neuk, and is a popular holiday area. There is pleasant cycling, although the road can be moderately busy. Crail became a Royal Burgh in 1310. Of interest is the Church of St Mary, dating from the 12thC, with a Pictish stone, and Crail Museum, which gives an insight into the town's history. (Free.)

Continue to Anstruther, where there is a great chip shop on the harbour front, and a hostel nearby. For route details between Anstruther and Elie, see Route 37. From Elie, go west on the A917 to Upper Largo, where the Scotland's Larder exhibition is of interest to foodies. It also has a restaurant, tel. 01333 360414. (Admission charge.)

Lower Largo is down from the main road. It is worth visiting Largo Bay, which has a nice beach and associations with Robinson Crusoe. The sailor Alexander Selkirk was born here in 1676, and returned after his ordeal on a desert island. Although Robinson Crusoe was shipwrecked, the real-life Selkirk, an irascible Scot, requested that he be put ashore on Juan Fernandez Island after quarrelling with the master of the Cinque Ports. He lived there for over four years before he was rescued by a privateer. The Crusoe Hotel, tel. 01333 320759, has a footprint of Man Friday cast in concrete (!) and other Selkirk memorabilia.

Not far round the coast lie the more industrial and less picturesque villages of Leven and Methil. Methil has few claims to fame except that Prince Philip, the Duke of Edinburgh, once described Methil as 'a right dump', and then told a local resident that it was 'a terrible place to live'. However, it should be pointed out that the towns are well liked by those who live there. The recommended route is to stick near the coast on the A955 to Kirkcaldy. The Kirkcaldy Art Gallery and Museum, tel. 01592 260732, has a good collection of Scottish artists. (Free.) On the Sailors' Walk are 17thC houses restored by the National Trust. At Dysart is the dramatic 15thC ruin of Ravenscraig Castle, and another nearby National Trust property is the John MacDouall Stuart Museum. Stuart was an explorer who opened up the overland telegraph route from South to North Australia in 1862. It had taken many years and the effort virtually killed him. He died in London in 1866 after returning blind and very sick with tropical diseases. (Free.)

The route passes through Burntisland, Aberdour and Inverkeithing to North Queensferry. Dalgety Bay is famed only for having a lot of radioactive paint littering the foreshore. Inverkeithing and North Queensferry, however, are pretty villages. At North Queensferry, Deep Sea World is a very popular attraction with aquaria and exhibitions, tel. 01383 411411. (Admission charges.) In South Queensferry is a museum which tells the history of the town and particularly of the queen's ferry. The queen in question is Queen Margaret, who died in 1093 and who encouraged pilgrims to travel to the shrine of St Andrew.

Near the famous Forth Rail Bridge, at Hawes Pier in South Queensferry, the cruise ship *Maid of the Forth* sails regularly to Inchcolm Island, where there is a well-preserved 12-14thC abbey, tel. 0131 331-4857/1451. The cruise offers a look at the magnificent cantilever rail bridge, built in 1890, which was renowned for being painted continuously. Now maintenance painting has been reduced and rusty lumps are falling off, absolutely safely according to the railway safety experts.

From South Queensferry the best way to cycle into Edinburgh is to take the disused railway track just east of Queensferry Museum to Dalmeny. The former rail route continues to near Carlowrie Farm, which is on Burnshot Road. From here proceed into Burnshot, and follow an improved path to Edinburgh Gate. A cycle path runs through Barnton Golf Course and joins the network of tracks and roads into Edinburgh. See OS map 65 for more details.

Route 35: Glen Clova Loop

See Fact Sheet 28 and first map for Route 34

The route leaves Kirriemuir and climbs up the quite hilly South Esk Valley. The B955 passes Cortachy Castle, and after about 4 miles the road splits. It doesn't matter which road you take as they both end up at the same place, and you can take the other road on the way back. The scenery up the glen is very pleasant and the river is good for sitting next to and soaking up the sun. At the top of the loop is the Clova Hotel, tel. 01575 550222, which does good bar food and has open fires. Carry on to Glendoll Hostel, which is a great base for hillwalking, and rather incongruously has a squash court for hyperactive residents. The route returns to Clova then back to Kirriemuir.

Route 36: Green Dundee Loop

See Fact Sheet 28

A useful leaflet is available from Dundee Tourist Information Office, which describes this 'Dundee Green Circular' route.

The route starts in the centre of Dundee near the road and rail bridges at Discovery Point where there is plenty of car parking. From here head west past the Vernonholme Botanic Gardens, part of Dundee University. Near here is the Mills Observatory, a Victorian centre for astronomy. This is the only council-owned observatory in Britain and is visited often by Patrick Moore. After Ninewells Hospital turn north (right) on tracks to the sports centre. Near here, on the other side of the Kingsway, is Shaws Sweet Factory, tel. 01382 461435, which has sweet-making demonstrations.

The route continues into Camperdown Country Park and heads north past the zoo to Camperdown House, which has a café. It then meanders through Templeton Woods and past Gallow Hill, continuing east through housing areas to Caird Park, where Mains Castle is situated with its restaurant. This is where the Dundee Highland Games are held every year in early July. Opposite is the Mains of Claverhouse pub, which has seats outside in summer.

The route continues round Dundee and out east to Monifieth, before turning and heading back towards the city along the beach. The Milton Hotel at Monifieth is recommended. At Broughty Ferry are various cafés, including the Fyffies Coffee Shop, and L'Auberge, both in Brook Street. But the best café has to be Vissochi's, an Italian restaurant which does excellent ice cream. There is also a museum at Broughty Castle detailing Dundee's whaling history. (Free.) Return to the centre of Dundee, staying south of the railway and off the busy Broughty Ferry Road. Where this ends, the unofficial route follows Port Road, which is fairly quiet, if industrial, back to the start point.

Route 37: East Fife Loop

See Fact Sheet 29 and second Map for Route 34

Start in the charming fishing village of Elie, where the harbour is worth visiting, not least because of the Ship Inn which serves the best pub grub I've ever tasted. It is a conservation area with lovely old houses that remind me of French villages. In fact, Anstruther, St Monans and Pittenweem all have different atmospheres. Anstruther is home of the excellent Scottish Fisheries Museum and the Anstruther Fish Bar on the harbour front. The museum, tel. 01333 311073, is on the site of the 15thC St Ayle's Chapel, and exhibits include old fishing boats in the harbour. There are boat trips to the Isle of May in the Firth of Forth which take 5 hours. Tel. 01333 310103.

The coast road can be a bit busy, so after Anstruther head northwest signposted to St Andrews, past West Pitkierie, where there is a hostel. Turn right on the B9171 and then left on the B940 to Scotland's Secret Bunker, tel. 01333 310301. This fascinating relic of the Cold War is 100 ft underground and was intended as a government command centre in the event of nuclear war. It has operations, communications and war-planning rooms, plus a café. (Admission charge.)

Continue along the B940 to the junction with the B9131 and at the next junction turn right back onto the B9171. This quiet road through farmland passes Kellie Castle, tel. 01333 720271, which is managed by the National Trust. (Admission charge.) The 16thC tower house was in poor repair when Sir James Lorimer leased it, and he and his son, the eminent architect Sir Robert Lorimer, restored it to its Scots Baronial splendour. The gardens were also restored and are very fine. The house exhibits the work and ideas of Sir Robert Lorimer, and has outstanding 17thC plaster ceilings and painted panelling. (Admission charge.)

From here the route continues west on the B9171, then on the B942, and the B941 through Kilconquhar back to Elie.

THE BORDERS

• •

The area south and east of Edinburgh has rolling hills and quiet roads, leading to the more fertile farmland approaching Berwick-upon-Tweed and England. The Borders are very pleasant, with magnificent ruins of abbeys and castles, and are famous for their association with the novelist Sir Walter Scott. This is another area which is off the beaten track for most tourists. However, it is more rewarding than most, particularly as there are many small roads which are ideal for cycling.

➤ **Route 38 (Grand Tour)**
Edinburgh-Berwick-upon-Tweed
♦♦ (♦) Moderate to strenuous. 62 miles.

➤ **Route 39 (Alternative Grand Tour)**
Edinburgh-Gretna
♦♦ (♦) Moderate to strenuous. 118 miles.

➤ **Route 40**
North Berwick Loop
♦♦ Moderate. 58 miles.

➤ **Route 41**
Three Abbeys
♦ (♦) Easy to moderate. 42 miles.

➤ **Route 42**
Biggar, Broughton & Dawyck Arboretum
♦ Easy. 18 miles.

➤ **Route 43**
New Lanark Loop
♦♦ Moderate. 26 miles.

➤ **Route 44**
Traquair Green Loop
♦ Easy. 16 miles.

➤ **Route 45**
Eyemouth & St Abbs
♦ Easy, with one steep hill. 15 miles.

➤ **Rail**
The East Coast Main Line runs from Edinburgh to Berwick-upon-Tweed via Dunbar, and on to London King's Cross. There is also a local line to North Berwick. Tel. 0345 484950 (enquiries) or 0345 550033 (bookings).

➤ **Cycle Tour Organizers**
   Traquair Bothy, in conjunction with Bike Sports in Innerleithen, offers a range of cycling holidays. Tel. 01896 830515/880.
   Scottish Borders Cycle Trails. Based in Peebles, they organize tours, both on- and off-road. Established and slightly impersonal. Tel. 01721 720336.

➤ **Tourist Information Offices (Open all year)**
   Berwick-upon-Tweed, Castlegate Car Park, tel. 01289 330733
   Dalkeith, The Library, White Hart Street, tel. 0131 663-2083
   Dunbar, 143 High Street, tel. 01368 863353
   Edinburgh, 3 Princes Street, tel. 0131 557-1700
   Gretna, Gateway to Scotland, M74 Service Area, tel. 01461 338500
   Hawick, Drumlanrig's Tower, tel. 01450 372547
   Jedburgh, Murray's Green, tel. 01835 863435/688
   Lanark, Horsemarket, Ladyacre Road, tel. 01555 661661
   North Berwick, Quality Street, tel. 01620 892197
   Pencraig, A1 by East Linton, tel. 01620 860063

➤ **Special Events**
   Hawick Common Riding, an ancient boundary-enforcing event, takes place in early June, while the Beer Festival at Traquair House near Innerleithen in May is good fun. The Traquair Music Fair takes place in August, as does the Berwickshire Agricultural Show at Mainsgate Park in Duns.

GRAND TOUR
Route 38: Edinburgh-Berwick-upon-Tweed

See Fact Sheet 30

Leave Edinburgh on the disused Innocent Railway, now a cycle path which runs round the back of the Commonwealth Pool, and south of Arthur's Seat. The Innocent Railway was one of the earliest railways, built between 1827 and 1831, from St Leonards to the collieries near Dalhousie. Originally wagons were pulled up the inclined plane into St Leonard's Depot, counterbalanced by descending trains. A passenger service using converted stagecoaches was later developed, in contrast to the more sophisticated steam locomotives. It was known as the Innocent Railway because of its pastoral and innocent appearance. There were no intermediate stations so passengers jumped on and off

East Lothian

Fact Sheet 30 ....

East Lothian, and particularly the area along the coast to North Berwick, is full of attractive villages inhabited by Edinburgh's commuters. This means that the roads tend to be busy. There is no satisfactory cycling route round the coast so the recommended Grand Tour route goes inland and over the Lammermuir Hills. The route then drops to the fertile plain around Berwick-upon-Tweed, where the Grand Tour ends and England begins.

➤ **OS Maps 66, 67, 74, 75**

➤ **Tourist Information Offices (Summer only)**
  Coldstream, High Street, tel. 01890 882607
  Eyemouth, Auld Kirk, Manse Road, tel. 01890 750678
  Newtongrange, Scottish Mining Museum, Lady Victoria Colliery,
  tel. 0131 663-4262

➤ **Cycle Shops**
  Neatworks, Guard Road Industrial Estate, Coldstream, tel. 01890 883456
  Cycle Services, Unit 2, Hospital Road, Haddington, tel. 01620 826989
  The Pennyfarthing, 23 Quality Street, North Berwick, tel. 01620 894400
  Wilson's Cycles, 17a Bridge Street, Berwick-upon-Tweed, tel. 01289 331476

➤ **Hostels**
  SYHA, Coldingham, Eyemouth, tel. 01890 771298
  SYHA, Abbey St Bathans, Duns, tel. 01361 840245

➤ **Banks**
  These are plentiful in North Berwick and Berwick-upon-Tweed, and can be found in many towns along the Forth estuary between Edinburgh and North Berwick.

➤ **Launderettes**
  Dandy Launderette, Bridge Street, Tranent, tel. 01875 614575

where they liked. The railway was sold in 1845 to the North British Railway for £133,000; the horses were pensioned off and the fearsome steam locos introduced, with a subsequent loss of innocence. The engine shed is now a café which serves wholesome home baking.

The railway's inclined plane makes for a rapid exit from Edinburgh. Another feature of interest is the cast-iron bridge over the Braid Burn which incorporates the earliest surviving inverted-'T' cross-section beams in the world. Duddingston Loch is full of ducks which

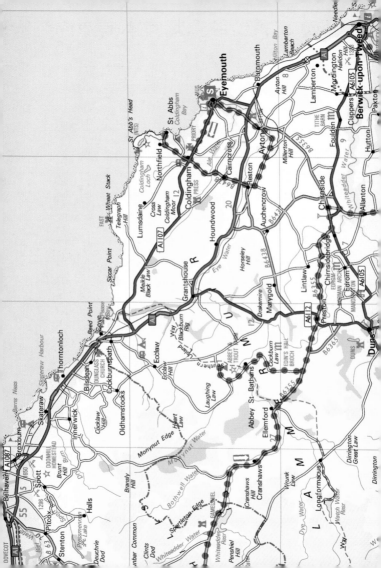

Edinburgh's toddlers come to feed. There is also a famous pub, the Sheep's Heid, tel. 0131 661-1020, which has good bar food and alfresco eating. James VI presented an embellished ram's head and horns to the hostelry, providing it with its present name.

The route continues to Portobello, and then through Musselburgh, where you should stop at Luca's for some great ice cream. Leave the coast and follow the River Esk Walkway to Pencaitland, on former railtracks now available for walking and cycling. Close by is Glenkinchie Distillery, on an unclassified road south of Pencaitland, which has visits by arrangement, tel. 01875 340333.

Head east to Gifford, and stay on the B6355 all the way to Chirnside. The Goblin Ha Hotel in Gifford, tel. 01620 810244, in the heart of Edinburgh's stockbroker belt, is good for alfresco pub grub and afternoon teas. The route leads over the Lammermuir Hills, which are heather-covered and splendid in late summer. Just past Whiteadder Reservoir is Cranshaw's Smithy, which serves much-needed tea. It is pretty crucial as this is the only tea and sandwich stop on the route. Otherwise, it is well worth bringing picnic food with you for this section. The small youth hostel in Abbey St Bathans is a good place to break your journey, although it is a slight detour. If you go there, the Riverside Restaurant, tel. 01361 840312, is good for meals or teas.

From Chirnside take the B6437 to Blackadder and then east into Berwick on the B6460. A detour on minor roads south of Paxton leads to Union Suspension Bridge, built over the Tweed in 1820 to connect Scotland with England, and the first of its type in Britain. Paxton House is a Georgian mansion with a tearoom. Built for the Home family, it was designed by the Adam brothers, and furnished by Chippendale. The art collection of Patrick Home is housed here. The house was gifted to the nation by John Home Robertson, Labour MP. The gallery is now part of the National Galleries of Scotland.

Care is required approaching Berwick-upon-Tweed as it is necessary to cross the busy A1. The town is now in England though in the past it has been hotly disputed over, changing hands 14 times between 1100 and 1500. There are impressive road and rail bridges over the mouth of the River Tweed, and these jostle for prominence with the town fortifications and the seafront. The castle is now in ruins but still features the Breakneck Stairs, while a cultural centre is housed in the Berwick Barracks, built in 1717 in another attempt to control the Jacobites. Both this route and the Grand Tour end here.

The Borders

Fact Sheet 31 . . . .

The Tweed Valley is long and meandering and runs through one of Scotland's sleepiest areas. It is a reasonably popular tourist destination, but mainly with the more discerning visitor who wants to escape the mad dash up to Loch Ness and the Highlands. Even so, the Borders are still very accessible from northern England and from the Scottish Central Belt, and are well worth exploring at leisure.

➤ **OS Maps 72, 73, 74**

➤ **Tourist Information Offices (Summer only)**
  Biggar, 155 High Street, tel. 01899 221066
  Eyemouth, Auld Kirk, Manse Road, tel. 01890 750678
  Galashiels, St John Street, tel. 01896 755551
  Kelso, Town House, The Square, tel. 01573 223464
  Melrose, Abbey House, tel. 01896 822555
  Peebles, High Street, tel. 01721 720138
  Selkirk, Halliwell's House, tel. 01750 20054

➤ **Cycle Shops**
  Scottish Borders Cycle Trails, Venlaw High Road, Peebles, tel. 01721 720336
  Bike Sports, 48 High Street, Innerleithen, tel. 01896 830880/831594
  George Pennel, 3 High Street, Peebles, tel. 01721 720844
  Cycling World, 53 Northgate, Peebles, tel. 01721 729549
  Gala Cycles, High Street, Galashiels, tel. 01896 757587
  Herbert Cycles, 5 Bridge Place, Galashiels, tel. 01896 755340

➤ **Hostels**
  SYHA, Melrose (Grade 1), tel. 01896 822521
  SYHA, Broadmeadows, near Selkirk, tel. 01750 76262
  SYHA, Kirk Yetholm, near Kelso, tel. 01573 420631
  Traquair Mill House and Bothy, Innerleithen, tel. 01896 830515

➤ **Banks**
  These can be found in Galashiels, Peebles, Hawick and Melrose.

➤ **Launderettes**
  ProntoClean, Nor Bridge, Hawick, tel. 01450 373131
  Washing facilities also available at Melrose SYHA (see above)

ALTERNATIVE GRAND TOUR
Route 39: Edinburgh-Gretna

See Fact Sheets 31 and 32

Instead of finishing the Grand Tour at Berwick-upon-Tweed on the east coast of Scotland, you may wish to return to Gretna, where the tour started. This route begins at Edinburgh, but it could also be done by following the Tweed Valley Cycle Route (see page 239) from Berwick-upon-Tweed to Innerleithen, near Peebles, and then heading south.

Stage 1: Edinburgh-Innerleithen

Leave Edinburgh heading south on the A701 over the Bridges by the Balmoral Hotel. Cross the High Street and at a roundabout bear right up Liberton Brae, passing close to the Royal Observatory on Blackford Hill. This road goes under the city bypass. Continue straight on, following signs for Penicuik and the A701. This road is fairly busy. Penicuik is quietly pleasant, but like many of the towns around here has suffered as mining and industry have declined. Edinburgh Crystal Visitor Centre, tel. 01968 673846, is housed in a former paper factory and has guided tours and demonstrations. Bear left and follow signs for Peebles on the A701.

Keep on the A701 and A703 south to Peebles, via Leadburn, where the Leadburn Inn does bar food. Peebles has a wide selection of eateries and is a popular place for afternoon tea. From Peebles take the B7062 towards Innerleithen. Details of the route here are given in the description for Route 44. At Traquair turn left for Innerleithen.

Stage 2: Innerleithen-Eskdalemuir

This route simply follows the B709 south, through the rolling hills of the Borders. There are some hilly sections, although these are not too extreme, and there are pubs at Mountbenger and Tushielaw which were originally drovers' inns. The Tushielaw Inn, tel. 01750 62205, is particularly popular with cyclists. Snoot Youth Hostel, tel. 01450 880259, a converted church covered in roses, is about 10 miles from the inn on the B711. ➤ 165

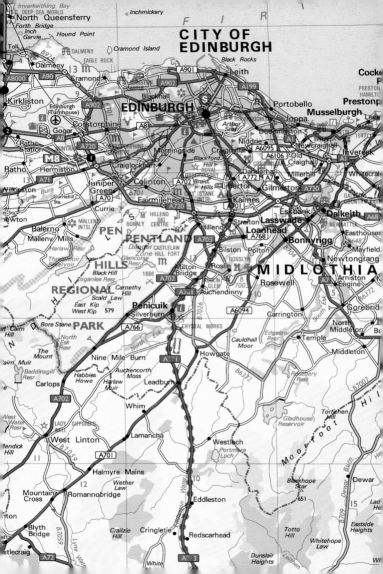

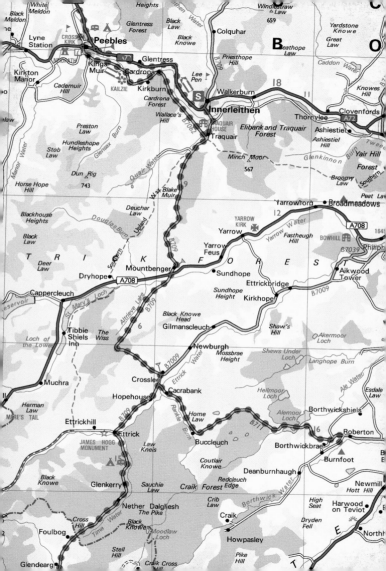

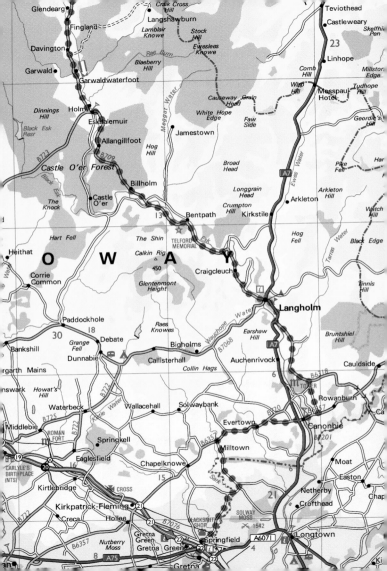

Fact Sheet 32 .... **Peebles & Gretna**

➤ **OS Maps 73, 79, 85**

➤ **Tourist Information Offices (Summer only)**
  Gretna Green, Old Blacksmith's Shop, tel. 01461 337834
  Langholm, High Street, tel. 01387 380976
  Peebles, High Street, tel. 01721 720138

➤ **Cycle Shops**
  Scottish Borders Cycle Trails, Venlaw High Road, Peebles, tel. 01721 720336
  Bike Sports, 48 High Street, Innerleithen, tel. 01896 830880/831594

➤ **Hostels**
  SYHA, Snoot, Roberton, Hawick, tel. 01450 880259
  Samye Ling Monastery, Eskdalemuir, tel. 01387 373232

➤ **Banks**
  All the Scottish and the main English banks are represented in Edinburgh.
  In addition, there are branches of the Scottish banks in Peebles and Gretna.

This is the heart of sheep country and at Ettrick a short diversion up the one and only side road leads to the monument to James Hogg, the Ettrick Shepherd. This contemporary of Sir Walter Scott's was his literary rival and a collector of local ballads. The area is famous for its sheep farming, but now huge tracts of forestry plantation have largely displaced the sheep. The route gets quite steep beyond the monument and rises to 1096 ft at the delightfully named Foulbog House.

Continue south towards Eskdalemuir, passing the fascinating Samye Ling Tibetan Monastery, which is signposted and pretty obvious, you will see people wandering around in orange robes. This is a real Tibetan monastery, and it is very friendly. A café is open Friday, Saturday and Sunday, and there is inexpensive accommodation of various sorts. Many people come here on retreat, to study Alexander Technique, take courses in yoga or just to enjoy the atmosphere. For more details, tel. 01387 373232. From here it is a couple of miles to Eskdalemuir.

Stage 3: Eskdalemuir-Gretna

Continue south on the B709 following the River Esk to Langholm. Langholm is a prosperous little town, built on the wealth of wool and tweed mills in the last century. It is also worth visiting Langholm Castle. The town is the birthplace of C.M. Grieve (Hugh Macdiarmid) and nearby is a monument to another local boy made good, the civil engineer Thomas Telford. The local Common Riding Celebrations in July buzz with life and horsemen charge round the town and up the hill.

The busy A7 doesn't make for pleasant cycling, but it is hard to avoid it completely. A mile from Langholm cross the Skipper Bridge over the River Esk and take the B6318 to Claygate. Then take two right turns to recross the Esk. Just before the main road is a parallel small road which leads into Canonbie. Canonbie has the excellent Riverside Inn, tel. 01387 371295, with great food and upmarket accommodation, which would make an excellent place to celebrate the end of your Grand Tour. You should book in advance, though, as it is very popular.

From Canonbie head west on the B6357 through Evertown. Turn left along a back road which follows the River Sark to Sarkhall. Cross the river and continue into Gretna. Gretna has always been a frontier town – a haven for outlaws, smugglers and runaway lovers – and the Old Smithy, where marriages were once 'forged', is now a museum with a self-service café.

◆ Route 40: North Berwick Loop

◆ See Fact Sheet 30 and first Map for Route 38

From Edinburgh, follow Route 38 along the Innocent Railway cycletrack to Musselburgh. OS map 66 is also useful, as there are many small tracks and back roads which may be used as pleasant diversions.

Musselburgh has the Scottish Mining Museum, tel. 0131 663-7519, housed in a former colliery which has, among other exhibits, a Cornish beam engine. Lady Victoria Colliery has been restored and there are guided tours. (Admission charge.) From Musselburgh, take the coast road west through Prestonpans and Cockenzie. Near Cockenzie is Preston Tower, which is a 15thC tower house. Details on access are posted on the gate.

At Longniddry there is a good place for pub grub, The Longniddry Inn. At Aberlady there is a lovely long beach which is excellent for bracing walks. The road is quite busy in places, especially on Sundays when it is popular with day-trippers from Edinburgh.

The village of Dirleton has a 13thC castle, now managed by Historic Scotland, with lovely gardens and a doocot (dovecote) in the grounds. There are yews surrounding the 17thC bowling green. (Admission charge.)

North Berwick should not be confused with Berwick-upon-Tweed, as they are a good distance apart. It is a nice little town, well known as a watering hole in summer for Edinburgh folk. Sadly the lovely out-door swimming pool here closed recently, but it is still nice to go and take the sea air. There are plenty of B&Bs here if you want to make this a weekend trip.

North Berwick is famous for its witchcraft trials of 1591, when many witches were condemned for plotting against King James VI. Visit North Berwick Museum, tel. 01620 824161, as well as Tantallon Castle further east, with its spectacular medieval keep, and views across to Bass Rock, tel. 01620 892727. (Admission charge.)

From North Berwick you could return to Edinburgh by train. Alternatively, head south on the B1347 to Athelstaneford and Haddington, then south on the B6369.

Near Athelstaneford is the Museum of Flight which has a range of exhibits from airships to jets and explains the history of aviation. Tel. 01620 880308. (Admission charge.) Haddington is an attractive town which has been restored with fine results. It is based on a medieval street plan and has nearly 300 buildings of architectural or historical merit. The Church of St Mary, next to the River Tyne, is where John Knox worshipped as a boy. The museum nearby is dedicated to the lives of Thomas Carlyle and his wife, the daugther of a Haddington doctor.

Near Haddington is Lennoxlove House, built to commemorate the Duchess of Lennox's love for her husband. It contains a fine collection of porcelain, portraits and furniture. The garden was laid out in the 17thC and has old roses and herbs. (Admission charge.) Follow Route 38 in reverse along the B6355 back to Edinburgh via the Innocent Railway.

Route 41: Three Abbeys

(◆) See Fact Sheet 31

The routes described here (41 and 42) take in part of the area covered by the Tweed Valley Cycle Route. This route is a nice idea, starting at the headwaters of the river and following it down to the coast. Sadly, the logistics of getting to the start point at Biggar, which is not on a railway, or back from the end point of Berwick-upon-Tweed, make it problematic. Instead I suggest a couple of loop tours in this area. There is much to do and plenty of scope for exploring.

Start at Melrose, one of the prettiest of the Borders towns. The first abbey in Melrose was founded in the 7thC by St Aidan. St Boswell was its second prior and St Cuthbert its third. This was something of a hat-trick! After the abbey was ransacked by Kenneth Macalpine, it was rebuilt in the 12thC. It is now a lovely ruin with graceful arches surrounded by nice teashops. Archaeologists have recently

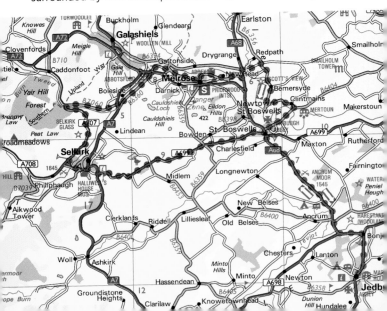

discovered a lead casket buried in the abbey ruins containing what is thought to be the heart of Robert the Bruce. (Admission charge.)

The route heads east from Melrose, crossing the Tweed at Leaderfoot to join the B6356 close to Scott's View. At Dryburgh, visit the abbey, romantically situated near the river. This is the burial site of Sir Walter Scott and Earl Haig. (Admission charge.)

The route heads west to Mertoun Bridge and into St Boswells via the B6404. Abbey enthusiasts may choose a diversion to Jedburgh to see a third splendid ruin. Alternatively, stick to the route which takes the busy-ish A699 to Selkirk. Sir Walter Scott, Sheriff of Selkirk, looks down from his pedestal on the town square. His courtroom is now open to the public. (Free.) Halliwell's House Museum has local history and changing exhibitions. (Free.) See also the 19thC Clapperton's Daylight Photographic Studio. (Admission charge.) There is a youth hostel in the town, and it is also the home of the delicious Selkirk Bannock, a sort of teacake.

Leave Selkirk on the A707 which is less busy than the main A7. Turn right after 2 miles to Sunderland Hall and cross the River Ettrick to join the A7 for a short distance. Follow the B6360 on the right bank to Abbotsford House, tel. 01896 752043, the home of Sir Walter Scott until his death in 1832. The splendid library has many thousands of books which Scott collected, and is currently being restored. His study with its leather-bound desk is very atmospheric. Among the remarkable contents of the house are the sword of Rob Roy and Bonnie Prince Charlie's hunting knife. Scott renamed his property Abbotsford because its previous name was Cartley Hall, itself a gentrified form of Clartyhole – 'clarty' meaning 'dirty' in Scots! Tearoom. (Admission charge.)

From here it is not far to return to Melrose, where the route ends. It has a splendid youth hostel, and various much-needed hostelries. A visit to Priorwood Garden on the A6091, a National Trust property, is pleasant. It specializes in drying flowers in sand using techniques developed by ancient Egyptians. (Admission charge.) Another delightful attraction is the Teddy Museum in Melrose. (Admission charge.)

Route 42:
Biggar, Broughton & Dawyck Arboretum
See Fact Sheet 33

The route starts in Biggar, a pleasant little market town, with a remarkable number of museums, all run by the Biggar Museum Trust. The Moat Park Heritage Centre tells the story of the local area and has a huge Victorian patchwork made by a local tailor during the Crimean War. (Admission charge.) The Biggar Gasworks Museum tackles the industrial heritage of the area and is housed in a former gasworks. (Free.) The Greenhill Covenanters House, tel. 01899 221050, is a restored farmhouse with displays on the 17thC Covenanters, as well as home to rare breeds of farm animals and poultry. Gladstone Court, tel. 01899 221050, has a street of Victorian shops, including a grocers, a chemists and a bank. Biggar Puppet Theatre has performances by the famous International Purves Puppets and nearby Brownsbank Cottage

Fact Sheet 33 · · · · · · · · · · · · · · · · · Biggar & Lanark

An interesting area of rolling hills and market towns, well worth spending time in, and especially handy for day trips from Edinburgh and Glasgow.

➤ OS Map 72

➤ Tourist Information Offices (Summer only)
Biggar, 155 High Street, tel. 01899 221066
Peebles, High Street, tel. 01721 720138

➤ Cycle Shops
Sandy's Bikes, 2 Wellgate Head, Lanark, tel. 01555 663315
George Pennel, 3 High Street, Peebles, tel. 01721 720844

➤ Hostel
SYHA, New Lanark, Wee Row, tel. 01555 666710

➤ Banks
Bank of Scotland, Bannatyne Street, Lanark, tel. 01555 662538

is the home of the great Scottish poet Hugh Macdiarmid. (Open by arrangement, tel. 01899 221050.)

From Biggar head east on the B7016 to Broughton. Just north of the village is Broughton Place, now a gallery for contemporary artists, which was designed by the controversial architect Sir Basil Spence in 1938 in the style of a traditional Scottish tower house. Outside are a knot garden and doocot (dovecote). Spence later went on to design a number of 'carbuncles', as well as buildings of great sensitivity such as Coventry Cathedral.

Continue east on an unclassified road to the junction with the B712. Turn left past Dawyck Arboretum, tel. 01721 6254, a fine garden run by the Royal Botanic Garden in Edinburgh. It has a collection of narcissi and rhododendrons, making it particularly attractive in spring.

Continue west past Tinnis Castle, and then join up with the A701, turning right back to Broughton. Just before the village, the John Buchan Centre, tel. 01899 221050, celebrates the author of *The Thirty-Nine Steps*, who was also Lord Tweedsmuir, Governor of Canada, soldier, historian and a gentleman. Broughton was his mother's birthplace and Buchan's favourite summer holiday home. (Admission charge.)

After 200 yd turn left on an unclassified road and proceed for a mile, bearing right at the next junction. Meander along until a sharp right turn takes you back towards Biggar.

Route 43: New Lanark Loop

See Fact Sheet 33 and Map for Route 42

Lanark is a centre for soft fruit- and tomato-growing in Scotland and has a regular agricultural market. The town has associations with William Wallace (1270-1305) who lived at Castlegate. Here he began his campaign of resistance to the English after his wife was killed by English soldiers. He murdered the Sheriff of Lanark and was declared an outlaw, and carried out a series of attacks on English castles and barracks. The uprising culminated in the Battle of Stirling Bridge, where the heavily outnumbered Scots defeated the English through their use of superior tactics. Eventually Wallace was captured, tortured and beheaded, but he led the way for Robert the Bruce. Mel Gibson's recent Oscar-winning film *Braveheart* has rekindled interest in Wallace.

New Lanark Visitor Centre, tel. 01555 661345, in the valley below the town, is a fascinating museum and tourist attraction which traces the legacy of the social reformer Robert Owen, who experimented with socially aware attitudes to workers. The industrial village of New Lanark was founded by David Dale in 1783, complete with a textile mill powered by the fast-flowing River Clyde. Soon the complex became one of Britain's major cotton mills. Dale employed orphans and migrant Highlanders, and in the 1790s over 1000 people were working here. Dale was a social engineer; he housed and paid his workers well, and educated them.

In 1800 Dale sold the mills to his son-in-law, Robert Owen, who is widely credited with the concept of New Lanark, but who built on Dale's principles. He raised the minimum age of employment to 12 and introduced other educational innovations, as well as a crèche. Owen went to America in 1824 and though New Lanark continued to trade, it gradually declined until 1967. Since then it has been restored by conservationists and is still a remarkable testimony to the ideals of its founders. (Free access to village. Admission charge for some of the attractions.)

The route leaves Lanark on the A72 and crosses the Clyde at Kirkfieldbank. Turn left immediately after the bridge to explore the Clyde Valley. The route alongside the river is partly on roads and partly on paths and passes through a spectacular gorge and past the Falls of Clyde. You emerge at a farm, Harperfield (GR 884397), from where a minor road heads up the Douglas Water towards Uddington.

For a short loop, take the first right on the B7078 and right again on the B7018 to complete a loop back to Kirkfieldbank.

An alternative longer route would be to continue past the junction of the B7078 with the B7018 to Blackwood, beyond Kirkmuirhill. A right turn on minor roads passes Craignethan Castle (admission charge), an impressive, well-preserved ruin which was once a stronghold of the Dukes of Hamilton, a couple of miles from Crossford, before returning to Kirkfieldbank. OS map 72 shows many minor roads in this area which are ideal for exploring by bicycle.

Route 44: Traquair Green Loop

See Fact Sheet 31 and second Map for Route 39

The A72 is the main obstacle on this green route. If you are intending to take children, take extra care. You may prefer just to explore the quiet B7062 road on the south bank of the Tweed.

Start at Innerleithen on the A72 and cycle towards Peebles, enjoying the views of the River Tweed. Glentress Forest to the right is popular with mountain bikers; leaflets are available from Forestry Commission or Tourist Information Offices. Various routes are waymarked.

Peebles is well-frequented by people having afternoon teas. Try the Sunflower, 4 Bridge Street. The town also has the most unlikely of museums, the Cornice Museum of Ornamental Plasterwork, tel. 01721 720212, being on Innerleithen Road. (Admission charge.)

The route heads across the River Tweed and east on the B7062, following the river back to Innerleithen through some extremely pleasant wooded scenery and farmland. Soon you come to Kailzie Gardens, which are open to the public. There is also a very superior café with wholesome food, guaranteed to boost flagging energy levels. Further on, you must visit Traquair House, tel. 01896 830323, the best stately home, I think, in Scotland. It is pleasingly eccentric, with melodramatic spider's webs and details of the prescriptions given to previous Maxwell lairds. The house has a brewery and another nice tearoom. It also has a particularly attractive wicker summerhouse. Special events and artwork displays often take place in the grounds and the estate is very much alive, rather than preserved in mothballs as some are. There is a music fair in early August. (Admission charge.) From Traquair it is a short cycle back to Innerleithen.

Route 45: Eyemouth & St Abbs

See Fact Sheet 34 and second Map for Route 38

Leave Eyemouth heading west on the A1107 to Coldingham. Eyemouth is a harbour town and the Eyemouth Museum, tel. 01890 750678, commemorates the horrific fishing disasier in which 189

Fact Sheet 34 . . . . **Eyemouth & St Abbs**

This area has lots of small roads which are ideal for cycling, as long as you stay off the dangerous A1. St Abbs is an attractive seaside village.

➤ **OS Map 67**

➤ **Tourist Information Office (Summer only)**
Eyemouth, Auld Kirk, Manse Road, tel. 01890 750678

➤ **Cycle Shops**
Wilson's Cycles, 17a Bridge Street, Berwick-upon-Tweed, tel. 01289 331476

➤ **Hostel**
SYHA, Coldingham, tel. 01890 771298

fishermen died, 129 of them from the town. The fishing fleet sailed out on a calm October day, only to be hit by a sudden storm. Of the 29 Eyemouth boats, only six survived. (Admission charge.) The town was a thriving smuggling centre in the 16thC, and many houses are said to have hidden passageways.

Coldingham has a good little pub, the Coldingham Inn, which has open fires when it is cold. St Abbs can be found at the end of the B6438 and is a pretty village perched on a cliff with attractive fishermen's cottages, now mainly holiday homes. A few lobster boats still work from here. Nearby is St Abbs Nature Reserve, with its huge colonies of guillemots, razorbills, kittywakes and terns on the spectacular cliffs. Behind the cliffs, Mire Loch supports a wide range of bird, insect and plant life, as well as hordes of rabbits. It is also worth walking along the beach to look at the bathing huts painted in bright primary colours. Walking north along the coast where puffins, guillemots and other seabirds breed on the cliffs is worthwhile. Cycling is not possible or allowed here – it is very dangerous.

From St Abbs, head south on the B6438 to Cairncross and on to Reston, taking care when crossing the A1. Turn left onto an unclassified road. At the next junction turn left on a dead straight road for 2 miles. Turn left again into Ayton, where it is worth visiting Ayton Castle, tel. 01890 781212. This is sometimes open to the public and is a fully restored and lived-in Victorian family home. From Ayton head north across a bridge over the A1 and back into Eyemouth.

OFF-ROAD & CHALLENGING ROUTES

This chapter brings together various arduous and fantastic routes, some of them involving wading through bogs and clambering over hills. You are warned that these routes could be distinctly dangerous in bad weather or if you are poorly equipped or inexperienced. Please be careful, and bear in mind that going into the hills always carries some danger. However, all the routes described here have been completed – and enjoyed.

➤ **Route 46**
Glen Affric
♦♦♦ Strenuous, and probably impossible in very wet weather. 39 miles.

➤ **Route 47**
Applecross Peninsula
♦♦♦ Strenuous. 97 miles.

➤ **Route 48**
Rob Roy Country
♦♦ Moderate mountain bike route. 41 miles.

➤ **Route 49**
Loch Katrine & the Trossachs
♦♦ Moderate, and quite hilly. 29 miles.

➤ **Route 50**
Callander, Dunblane & Doune
♦♦ Moderate mountain bike route. 42 miles.

➤ **Route 51**
Loch Tay
♦♦ Moderate, and quite hilly. 47 miles.

➤ **Route 52**
Oban-Braemar Cross-country
♦♦♦ Strenuous mountain bike route. 118 miles.

For further details, see the appropriate fact sheets.

CHAPTER 10

Route 46: Glen Affric

See Fact Sheet 35

Note that this route is best tackled travelling as lightly as possible. However, a sleeping bag and sufficient food should be carried, and appropriate OS maps and a compass are essential.

The route starts at Shiel Bridge, at the head of Loch Duich, and near to Ratagan Youth Hostel. Head northeast up the glen on forestry tracks. Either take the footpath on the right bank, or take the much better forestry track on the left. However, if you take the forestry track, you have to cross the river. It is best to cross high up where the river peters out, but this is a bit of a scramble. Refer to OS map 33.

At the head of Strathcroe the track turns east and then southeast over the Bealach an Sgairne. This was the track taken by Bonnie Prince Charlie, and nearby are caves where he hid from his English pursuers. From here drop down to the south end of the delightful Loch a' Bhealaich. This land is owned by the National Trust for Scotland.

From here continue west for about 4 miles, along Allt Gleann Gniomhaidh. Initially this involves a small rise and then following the north bank of the burn. In places this can get very boggy and the path is a bit hit and miss. It depends on how much rain there has been, but it is do-able.

On reaching the River Affric, turn east (left) to reach Alltbeithe Youth Hostel, close to a bridge. Stay here overnight. It is a great place.

From here the route continues east. The path soon turns into a Landrover track and markedly improves. The Glen Affric Estate was once earmarked as a place for a national park but that has never materialized. Fine native woodlands in this area have suffered through overgrazing by deer and insensitive commercial forestry plantings. Recently the Trees for Life charity, based at the Findhorn Foundation, carried out some remedial work. This has been matched by the Forestry Commission which has carried out work to protect native Scots pines. The western part of Glen Affric has recently been taken over by the National Trust for Scotland.

Continue east on the south side of Loch Affric, then drop down Glen Affric, past stunning Loch Beinn a'Mheadhoin, where some of the best

Fact Sheet 35

Glen Affric

The route climbs up from Glen Shiel. The first part is basically on footpaths and is cycle-able by experienced mountain bikers only. However, you can walk! OS map 33 is absolutely essential. The path heads over the Bealach an Sgairne and down to the south end of Loch a'Bhealaich. From there the path along Gleann Gniomhaidh is boggy, but you cannot get lost. There is a wonderful youth hostel at Alltbeithe. Make sure you take lots of food and midge repellent in summer with you so you can stay for days! Booking in advance may be sensible. From here the track improves dramatically and you can cycle all the way down Glen Affric.

➤ OS Maps 25, 33

➤ Tourist Information Office (Summer only)
Shiel Bridge, tel. 01599 511264

➤ Cycle Shops
For nearest, see Inverness (Fact Sheet 19) and Kyleakin (Fact Sheet 13).

➤ Hostels
SYHA, Ratagan, near Shiel Bridge, tel. 01599 511243
SYHA, Glen Affric. No phone. Bring own bedding. OS 079202
SYHA, Cannich, near Beauly, tel. 01456 415244

➤ Hotel
Glen Affric Hotel, Cannich, tel. 01456 415214

➤ Banks
The nearest banks are in Inverness.

➤ Launderette
At Ratagan Youth Hostel (see above).

Scots pines in Scotland can be seen, as well as other species. This is a particularly fine place to visit in the autumn. Referring to the OS map shows various forestry tracks south of the loch. These make excellent mountain bike loops from the car park at the top of the glen. From Cannich there are two alternatives. Either take minor roads northeast to Beauly to join Route 23 or go east on the A831 through Glen Urquhart to Drumnadrochit on Loch Ness to join Route 21.

◆ Route 47: Applecross Peninsula

◆ See Fact Sheet 36
◆

This route consists of some of Scotland's best and most demanding cycling. The roads on the West Coast tend to be quite hilly, and the Bealach na Ba over to Applecross, at 2053 ft, is a challenge for only really fit people to cycle. However, it is easy enough to walk up. The perils are complete agony and being drenched with sweat, while the rewards are an irrational sense of achievement and superb views.

To get to the start of the route at Plockton from Kyle of Lochalsh, follow the directions given in Route 17. The road from Plockton is hilly, and the vegetation has a density and greenness which is subtropical. It passes the wonderful sign for Stromeferry, under which someone

Fact Sheet 36 . . . . **Applecross Peninsula**

The main attraction, if that is the right word, is the fantastic Bealach na Ba – the Pass of the Cattle - which climbs dramatically from sea level to just over 2000 ft. This is the highest and steepest mountain pass in Scotland, and the surrounding mountains are extraordinarily atmospheric. The reward for the climb is the marvellous descent to Applecross, which has a nice pub and is a delightful place, with great views to Raasay and Skye.

➤ OS Map 24

➤ Tourist Information Office
Lochcarron, Main Street, tel. 01520 722357

➤ Cycle Shops
For nearest, see Kyleakin (Fact Sheet 13).

➤ Hostel
The nearest is SYHA, Torridon, Achnasheen, tel. 01445 791284.

➤ Banks
The nearest is at Kyle of Lochalsh (see Fact Sheet 13).

➤ Launderette
Torridon Youth Hostel (see above).

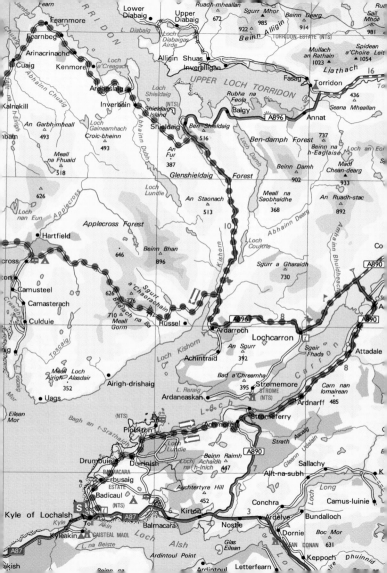

has written 'No ferry', which is a pity as it would save a few miles. This is one of the prettiest little roads, but it is overshadowed by some spectacular overhanging cliffs with none too reassuring road signs warning of falling boulders. There are also patches of Caledonian pine, oak and birch. After a pot of tea at the Strathcarron Hotel, tel. 01520 722227, my companion and I set off again along the A896. He took this jolly seriously, but then he had cycled all the way from Ayr to cycle up this 'pimple'. The hills of Beinn Bhan and Meall Gorm are squat, mean-looking mountains, and there was quite a hard headwind blowing from the west. The climb is steep up Bealach na Ba and follows the right-hand shoulder above the glen, before negotiating three zigzags and reaching the summit at 2053 ft. I was completely exhausted by the time I reached the top, but there was Steve, nonchalently reading his book in the mist. We put on all available warm clothes before whizzing down to Applecross to get fed before the kitchen closed at the Applecross Hotel, tel. 01520 744262. Applecross and the surrounding area have always been remote and in the past relied on transport by water. St Maelrubha founded a religious community here c.AD 670 but this was destroyed by the Vikings and nothing now remains except some slabs in the graveyard. The remains of a 15thC church are also visible.

The route from Applecross is now quite straightforward and follows the coast north. The scenery and views of Skye are the main attraction. Stop at Shieldaig, at the wonderful Rivendell, tel. 01520 755250. Yes, there is a copy of *Lord of the Rings* in every room. It also gets my vote as the tea stop with the best open fire, as well as doing B&B and laundry. Then it is up Glen Shieldaig and back past Kishorn, an oilrig fabrication yard which is now closed, to Lochcarron, then on to Achintee for trains to Inverness, or return to Plockton and on to Kyle of Lochalsh.

◆ Route 48: Rob Roy Country

◆ See Fact Sheet 37

The area on the east side of Loch Lomond is one of the most beautiful in Scotland. The road on the west of Loch Lomond is a disaster for cycling, and indeed for the loch itself. It has been much improved and now carries heavy traffic, making it thoroughly unpleasant.

Fact Sheet 37

Rob Roy Country

This route connects with Route 9 from Strachur, via Arrochar. However, the connecting route involves some busy roads, and a vicious hill – The Rest and Be Thankful. Alternatively, get to Inveruglas, north of Tarbet, by train to Arrochar on the West Highland Line, then cycle up the A82 alongside Loch Lomond.

➤ **OS Maps 56, 57**

➤ **Tourist Information Offices**
Callander, Rob Roy and Trossachs Visitor Centre, tel. 01877 330342
Dumbarton, A82 Northbound, Milton, tel. 01389 742306
Killin, Main Street, tel. 01567 820254 (summer only)
Tarbet (Loch Lomond), Main Street, tel. 01301 702260 (summer only)

➤ **Ferries**
Inveruglas-Inversnaid Hotel, Loch Lomond (summer only).
Tel. 01877 386223
Stronachlachar-Trossachs Pier, Loch Katrine (summer only), operated by the steamship *Sir Walter Scott*.
Tel. 01877 376315. A pleasant trip from Stronachlachar to the heart of the Trossachs.
Inverbeg-Rowardennan, Loch Lomond.
Tel. 01360 870273

➤ **Cycle Shops**
Trossachs Holiday Park, 4 miles south of Aberfoyle, tel. 01877 382614. Bike hire, spares and repairs.
Outdoor Centre and Mountain Shop, Killin, tel. 01567 820652. Bike hire and repairs.

➤ **Hostels**
SYHA, Killin, tel. 01567 820546
SYHA, Crianlarich, tel. 01838 300260
SYHA, Rowardennan, tel. 01360 870259

➤ **Banks**
There are banks in Callander an also further afield in Stirling.

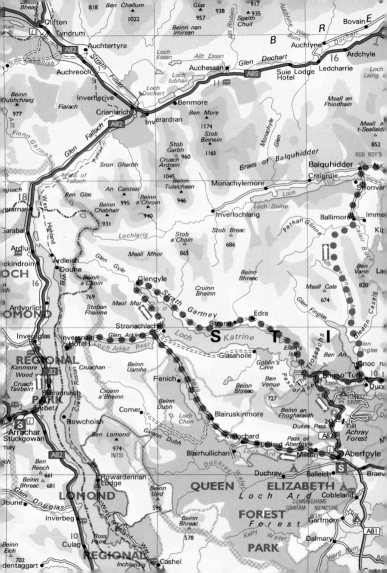

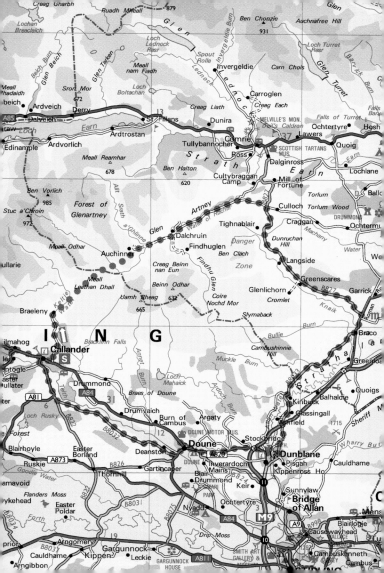

Fortunately, there is no east bank equivalent, as the road to Rowardennan is a cul-de-sac. The route continues north as part of the West Highland Way but this is not completely cycle-able, and anyhow cycling is discouraged. Even so, it is possible to get to Inversnaid.

Take the train to Arrochar and cycle through Tarbet on the busy A82 north to Inveruglas. From here catch the ferry to Inversnaid, where there is a hotel. Climb up the glen beside Loch Arklet, part of a hydro-electric dam complex, and continue to Stronachlachar which is served by a little steamboat, the *Sir Walter Scott* (April-October).

Head northeast from Stronachlachar along the cycle track and follow the route round the banks of Loch Katrine. This loch has supplied water to Glasgow since 1859. At the west end of Loch Katrine is Glen Gyle, where Rob Roy (see feature on page 188) was born, and where he reputedly held stolen cattle.

From Loch Katrine the road is good and after a mile you emerge by Loch Achray. Continue west for a couple of miles to Brig o' Turk, where there is a great café. Two choices then present themselves. The simplest is to head east on the A821 to Callander then head north on the purpose-built Sustrans route on the west side of Loch Lubnaig through Strathyre and into Balquhidder.

An alternative, and wilder, route into the heart of Rob Roy Country, for which OS map 57 is essential, heads north from Brig o' Turk, forking right and round Glen Finglas Reservoir to Creag na Croiteige, from where you should head north. At first this is quite a reasonable route but it deteriorates to a footpath. Cross a pass, Bealach a' Chonnaidh, then swing to the east and cross the burn at a bridge (GR 529175), before dropping down on a metalled road to Balquhidder.

Balquhidder has a lovely graveyard where Rob Roy is buried, and the local congregation have been offering teas and home baking to visitors following the successful film of *Rob Roy*. This caused a certain amount of chagrin to local teashop owners. The Bygones Museum in the Laird's baronial mansion has an official tearoom.

From Balquhidder you could return towards Callander on the Sustrans route south and back to Brig o' Turk to complete a good loop.

However, there are two other choices. A rough route north eventually joins up with the busy A85, from where you should head west to

Crianlarich to catch the train south. A Sustrans route is planned on the disused railtrack up Glen Ogle, and this should soon be in place. The A85 up Glen Ogle is not particularly cyclist-friendly, but it does lead to Killin and Loch Tay, which makes the trip worthwhile.

Route 49: Loch Katrine & the Trossachs

See Fact Sheet 38 and Map for Route 48

Aberfoyle is a pleasant village which is popular for Sunday afternoon runs out from Glasgow, and is well equipped with pubs, eating establishments and gift shops. It is also the B&B capital of the Trossachs, the name given to the surrounding hills which are covered in heather, as well as silver birch, rowan and the ubiquitous Sitka spruce. In the novel *Rob Roy* by Sir Walter Scott, Aberfoyle is the home of the hero Baillie Nicol Jarvie. The Scottish Wool Centre has presentations on

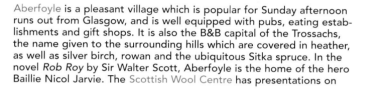

Fact Sheet 38   **Loch Katrine & the Trossachs**

One of the best one-day rides on quiet roads through scenery which is picturebook alpine. It is not a difficult ride but it is very satisfying. Part of the route follows directions given for Route 48. There are few tourist facilities so take your own food and drink.

➤ **OS Maps 56, 57**

➤ **Tourist Information Office (Summer only)**
Aberfoyle, Main Street, tel. 01877 382276

➤ **Ferry**
Sir Walter Scott, Loch Katrine, tel. 01877 376315
Phone in advance for times from Stronachlachar and Loch Katrine Pier.

➤ **Cycle Shops**
Trossachs Holiday Park, 4 miles south of Aberfoyle on the A81, tel. 01877 382614

➤ **Banks**
Bank of Scotland, Main Street, Aberfoyle, tel. 01877 382747

the history of sheep and shepherding and features live specimens. It also has spinning and weaving, and occasional sheep-dog trials. (Admission charge.) On the other side of the Forth the kirkyard contains the ruins of the old kirk as well as a number of cast-iron mortesafes, designed to prevent grave-robbing. Aberfoyle is in the Queen Elizabeth Forest Park, and on the hill above the town is the park's visitor centre, the David Marshall Lodge.

Leave Aberfoyle on the B829 and head through Milton, a conservation village, then past Loch Ard and Loch Chon, with tremendous views ahead to Ben Lomond, and on to Stronachlachar. At Stronachlachar turn left and follow the cycle track around Loch Katrine, the setting for Sir Walter Scott's ballad *The Lady of the Lake*, written in 1810. The loch supplies excellent-quality water to Glasgow via a series of tunnels, and Glen Gyle at the head of the loch is where the outlaw Rob Roy (see feature) was born.

The attractions of this area are simple: wonderful scenery and no traffic. About a mile beyond the east end of the loch, turn right on the busy and winding A821 over the Duke's Pass. This steep pass goes through the Trossachs and drops back down into Aberfoyle.

ROB ROY

Robert Macgregor (1671-1734), known as Rob Roy or the Red Macgregor, was a local clan chief. An outlaw, cattle thief and brigand, he was romanticized and turned into a folk hero by Sir Walter Scott in his novel *Rob Roy* of 1818. The recent film starring Liam Neeson reinforced this view. In fact Rob Roy was the son of Lieutenant-Colonel Donald Macgregor of Glenorchy and therefore a minor member of the Scottish aristocracy. In 1711 he raised £1000 on a credit note issued by the Duke of Montrose and his drover absconded with it. Rob Roy was accused of embezzlement and had to go into hiding on land near Killin provided by the Earl of Breadalbane, an enemy of the Montroses.

Macgregor relied on sheep- and cattle-rustling from lowland farms, particularly on Montrose estates, to earn his living. He twice wriggled out of arrest by Government forces but in 1725 he submitted to General Wade and received a King's Pardon. He died in 1734 at his home at Inverlochlarig at the head of Balquhidder Glen and is buried next to his wife in Balquhidder graveyard. The inscription on the stone reads 'Macgregor despite them', a reference to the fact that the name was banned three times between the 16th and 18thC.

Route 50: Callander, Dunblane & Doune

See Fact Sheet 39 and Map for Route 48

Start in Callander, a pretty, but very busy town northwest of Stirling. The Rob Roy Visitor Centre at the Tourist Information Office has an audiovisual presentation about the celebrated outlaw and the surrounding area. (Admission charge.) The route goes off-road and OS map 57 is essential.

 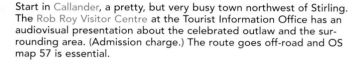

Callander, Dunblane & Doune

An excellent area for family holidays, with rich farmland, plenty of back roads, forests and interesting little towns and villages well supplied with hotels and coffee shops.

➤ **OS Map 57**

➤ **Tourist Information Offices**
Crieff, Town Hall, High Street, tel. 01764 652578
Callander, Ancaster Square, tel. 01877 330784 (summer only)
Dunblane, Stirling Road, tel. 01786 824428 (summer only)

➤ **Cycle Shops**
R.S. Finnie, Leadenflower Road, Crieff, tel. 01764 652599
Crieff Mountain Bike, 66 Commissioner Street, Crieff, tel. 01764 654667
Wildcat Mountain Activities, 15a Henderson Street, Bridge of Allan,
tel. 01786 832321

➤ **Banks**
Branches of the main Scottish banks can be found in Callander and Crieff.

➤ **Launderettes**
Washing Well, Station Road, Callander, tel. 01877 330667

Head north from Callander up the Keltie Water and cross the foot-bridge. Branch off at Arivurichardich (GR 643137) and continue east to Glen Artney. Continue down the valley and keep turning to the right to reach the B827 to Braco. Nearby, and signed from the village, is Ardoch Roman Fort, dating from the 1st and 2ndC AD.

Continue south on the B8033 west of the River Allan to Dunblane, a pleasant town with some graceful buildings. Dunblane Cathedral dates from the 13thC but was restored in the 19thC. (Free.) Turn right on the A820 to Doune.

Doune is a most attractive village, entered by a bridge over the River Teith originally built in 1535 and paid for by Robert Spittall, James IV's tailor, supposedly after the ferryman had refused him passage. Doune Castle was built at the end of the 14thC and is one of the best-preserved in Scotland. Built for the Duke of Albany, Regent of Scotland during the minority of James I, it contains an impressive gatehouse tower and combines defensive needs with elegance and comfort. (Admission charge.) Doune became known in the 17thC for the manufacture of pistols. Just northwest of the village on the A84 is the Doune Motor Museum, tel. 01786 841203, the Earl of Moray's collection of vintage cars, including the second-oldest Rolls Royce in the world. There is a tearoom. (Admission charge.) Back in the vil-lage, cross the River Teith and head up the south bank towards Callander on the B8032. Go to the end of this road and turn right onto the A81 for a couple of miles back to Callander.

◆ Route 51: Loch Tay

◆ **See Fact Sheet 40**

The route starts in Killin, a lovely alpine village, where the Falls of Dochart are a good place to pause and watch the salmon struggling upstream to spawn. If you are a horror-lover you could seek out the ruined Finlarig Castle, which has a beheading pit. Head east from Killin on the A827 for about 5 miles and take the steep road north signposted for Ben Lawers and Glen Lyon.

The road climbs to over 1800 ft and is one of the tougher hill climbs. At the Ben Lawers Visitor Centre you can learn about the wildlife of

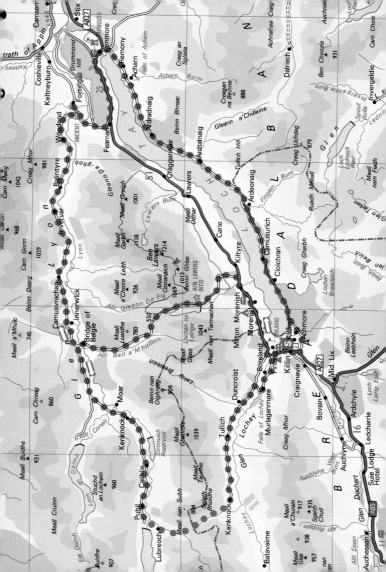

Loch Tay

Fact Sheet 40 . . . .

A magnificent area at the heart of the Scottish Highlands, with beautiful lochs and pretty villages. At Fortingall, reputed to be the birthplace of Pontius Pilate, is an ancient yew tree.

➤ **OS Map 51**

➤ **Tourist Information Offices**
Aberfeldy, The Square, tel. 01887 820276
Killin, Main Street, tel. 01567 820254 (summer only)

➤ **Hostels**
SYHA, Killin, tel. 01567 820546
Bunkhouse, Dunolly House, tel. 01887 820298. Also offers bike hire.
Bunkhouse, Mains of Kenmore, Kenmore, tel. 01887 830226

the mountain, which is a nature reserve on account of its botanical significance. There is no tearoom so take a picnic. The placing of this visitor centre was controversial and the National Trust for Scotland has been criticized for encouraging visitors. Mountain biking on the hills here is strongly discouraged.

Continue on the road to the summit cairn north of Lochan na Lairige. As you start to descend you pass a mass of sheilings where cattle-herds once lived.

Drop down to Bridge of Balgie and cross the River Lyon. Here you can admire the classic U-shaped valley created by glaciation. Glen Lyon is the supposed home of the legendary Finn MacCool, who had a number of castles along the glen, now just rough piles of rocks. (If you have time it is worth heading up the glen to the dam and hydro-electric scheme at Loch Lyon. There is a wild route back to Killin from here which takes the road south to Kenknock in Glen Lochay.)

Glen Lyon is very pleasant and you should see Carnbane Castle and Macgregor's Leap, where Rob Roy jumped to freedom from Government soldiers. There is much magnificent woodland and good places for picnics. At the road-end turn left and visit Fortingall, where there is an ancient if bedraggled Yew Tree, thought to be 2000-3000 years old, which is linked to Pontius Pilate, who supposedly was born here. The village is part of the Glen Lyon estate and has thatched cottages which give it more of a feel of Somerset than Scotland.

From Fortingall return to Bridge of Lyon and head south to Fearnan, then head east on the A827 along the banks of Loch Tay for about 3 miles. This area is well provided with B&B and hotel accommodation. Kenmore is another village planned by the Glen Lyon estate, and the Kenmore Hotel, tel. 01887 830205, is Scotland's oldest pub, having been built in 1572.

From Kenmore take the little road on the south bank of Loch Tay. A mile or so along at Croft na Caber is a watersports centre which organizes rafting on the nearby River Tay. There is also a teashop. Next to it is an interesting project which is re-creating a life-size crannog – a stilt dwelling situated in the loch – as part of an archaeo-logical project studying the 18 Bronze-Age crannogs on the loch. Nearby, a dug-out canoe and other remains have been discovered. Further on the Ardeonaig Hotel does afternoon teas.

Continue west to Killin along the banks of Loch Tay in the shadow of Ben Vorlich and with wonderful views back across the loch towards Ben Lawers.

Route 52: Oban-Braemar Cross-country

See Fact Sheet 41

A superbly satisfying route through some of Scotland's wildest scenery, combining serious off-road cycling with pushing and carrying and some roads. It took me 4 days' cycling, plus a night in Casualty! Please regard this as a cautionary tale. Do as I say and not as I do.

Glen Kinglass, Glen Tilt and Rannoch Moor are so remote that you feel sorry for the folk trudging along the West Highland Way, not to men-tion travelling on the roads. You will see a cross-section of Scotland in miniature, from the West Coast, to the mountains of Glencoe, and the much more fertile, tree-covered highlands of Perthshire. Then it's through Royal Deeside, past Balmoral, and down to Aberdeen. The route depends on a reasonable degree of fitness, common sense and the ability to use maps and compass, and don't do it alone, like I did. Rannoch Moor is fine lightly loaded, but could be hellish with too much gear, or if the weather has been really wet. Despite this being a classic mountain bike route, I used my road tourer, which was fine. If you are frightened of getting lost, bring distress flares and if you are worried about falling off your bike, wear a helmet.

Oban–Braemar

Fact Sheet 41

This is an extremely satisfying route for fit cyclists travelling light. The path across Rannoch Moor can be very muddy if there has been much rain – and that is normal. The route takes in much of Scotland's varied scenery, from the rugged West Coast to Braemar in the heart of Royal Deeside. OS maps and a compass, and the ability to use them, are vital. This route is potentially hazardous for those inexperienced in the conditions and weather of the Scottish hills.

➤ **OS Maps 42, 43, 49, 50**

➤ **Tourist Information Offices**
Braemar, The Mews, Mar Road, tel. 01339 741600
Oban, Argyll Square, tel. 01631 563122
Pitlochry, 22 Atholl Road, tel. 01796 472215
Tyndrum, Main Street, tel. 01838 400246 (summer only)

➤ **Cycle Shops**
For Oban, see Fact Sheet 5.
Blair Atholl Activity Cycles, Old School Park, Blair Atholl, tel. 01796 473553. Bike hire.
Braemar Mountain Bike Centre, 15 Mar Road, Braemar, tel. 01339 741242

➤ **Hostels**
SYHA, Oban, The Esplanade, tel. 01631 562025
SYHA, Inverey, 5 miles west of Braemar. No telephone
SYHA, Braemar, Corrie Feragie, 21 Glenshee Road, Braemar, tel. 01339 741659

➤ **Remote Hotels**
Inveroran Hotel, near Bridge of Orchy, tel. 01838 400220
Kingshouse Hotel, Glencoe, tel. 01855 851259
Rannoch Hotel, by Rannoch Station, tel. 01882 633238

➤ **Banks**
The nearest are in Oban (Fact Sheet 5). Otherwise, there are none until Braemar.

➤ **Launderettes**
At Oban and Braemar Youth Hostels (see above).

Stage 1: Oban-Inveroran

I set off from Oban with a friend on a misty day. We climbed the steep hill out of town amid heavy traffic, then followed the shore northwards. The smell of the sea was overpowering. Dunstaffnage Castle, tel. 01631 562465, 4 miles north of Oban, is a fine 13thC castle on a rock at the entrance to Loch Etive. It is still lived in but visitors are welcome. (Admission charge.)

At Connel Bridge the Falls of Lora are a tidal rip which flows like a river. The roadside was crammed with wild strawberries which tasted amazing, although doubtless were covered in lead. We turned off a couple of miles after Taynuilt on a road signposted to Inverawe Smokehouse, taking a forestry track 200 yd after two new buildings. If you get to the smokehouse you've gone too far. However, it does have a public display, and you can buy salmon.

The forestry track is very cycle-able, and we rolled along happily. There is only one junction, where you should bear left and stay near the shore of Loch Etive. The area teems with birds, and we saw lots of buzzards, eagles, and many seabirds. However, the overwhelming sense is that of smell: the pine trees with their pungent sweet scent, the bracken, the wild thyme and the honeysuckle.

Turn into Glen Kinglass, crossing a new wooden bridge, then turning right along a track that follows the burn. It is a good Landrover track which climbs steadily without many problems to Glen Kinglass Lodge. This is a long grassy valley, part of the estate owned by the Fleming family, of which Ian Fleming, creator of James Bond, was a part. By the lodge a rock is painted with a red stag, like a Neolithic cave painting. It is also near the home of Francis Fleming, who has written a rather good mountain biking book (Mountain Biking in the Scottish Highlands), though curiously he left out this route.

The track deteriorates as it reaches then goes over the watershed. There is a very narrow bridge and the views of Ben Starav and Stob Garbh are stunning. We soon rejoined a reasonable track, and reached Loch Dochard. There are some trees here, which makes a change, and then the River Dochard has to be forded.

The track then continues to Inveroran. This area gets overrun with walkers doing the West Highland Way, so booking in advance is advisable. The food at the Inveroran Hotel is good and the beer is even better.

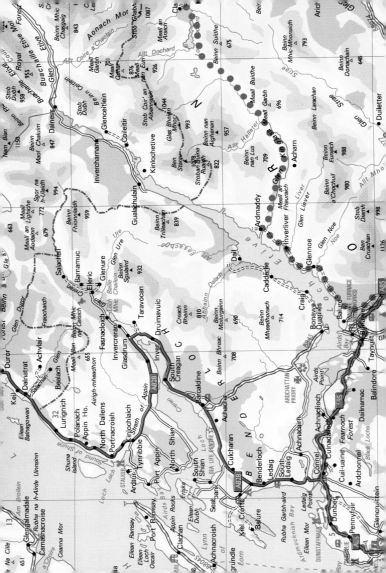

Stage 2: Inveroran-Loch Rannoch

We left Inveroran at 10.30 on an exceptionally rainy day. We had the wind in our faces and spent the first hour dodging the hordes of people trudging along the West Highland Way. The WHW is very much a walking route and not recommended for cycling, and indeed bikes are discouraged. However, this section is OK as it has been used for cycling since long before the WHW or indeed mountain bikes were invented.

Rannoch Moor is a high wet plateau covered in peat and water and the roots of ancient trees which once covered the area. The road we followed was built by General Wade to suppress the Scots after the 1715 rebellion. The track is quite cycle-able, but is deteriorating because of erosion.

Ba Bridge is beautiful and a lovely place to camp. The Ba River runs through a gorge studded with primroses. We passed the memorial cairn to Peter Fleming – Ian's brother – and finally emerged at the ski road next to Blackrock Cottage, before zooming down the wet tarmac to Kingshouse Hotel, near the mouth of Glencoe, which claims to be Scotland's oldest hotel.

After lunch I continued alone, my companion having returned to civilization, in the form of his warm flat, wife and guitar. I admit I was reluctant, and was not helped by the predictions of those who said the track barely existed. Don't believe such sceptics – the reality is that a track certainly does exist, even if it's not great. Just north of the hotel a large metal sign announces a public footpath to Rannoch.

The first 4 miles to Black Corries Lodge is a good track. Beyond the lodge the track gradually deteriorates into a footpath, and it is then a 2 hour walk until you enter a forestry plantation.

In compensation the rain abruptly stopped, though heavy rain clouds still hung over Kingshouse and Glencoe. Both the rain and midges of Rannoch are legendary, but it was amazing how obvious was the divide between the wet west and the much drier east. It is almost inevitable that you will get muddy, and there were also huge cowpats, which were something of a surprise. There was an owl hunting on the hillside and a fair number of ducks and other birds on Loch Laidon. I met a Dutch couple walking the other way, and we had a Dr Livingston-type discussion.

At one point I sank into the slimy peat up to my knees, and as I wallowed I remembered the skeleton which was discovered out here of one of the Irish navvies who built the railway line across the bog. He was found rather well preserved, still clutching his whisky bottle.

At 5 pm I got my first glimpse of a house, and after a few more boggy bits, turned up a steep hill and found a forestry track, which I could actually cycle on. I arrived at Rannoch Station tearoom as the clock struck six. The tearoom shuts at six! Fortunately there is a bar at the Rannoch Hotel where you can get food and beer. There is not much accommodation though. The hotel is pricey and was full, so I pressed on to a guest house about 12 miles away, on the north shore of Loch Rannoch. The road down from Rannoch Station is completely different from the bleakness of Rannoch Moor. Suddenly there are beautiful trees, and cottages with roses climbing up the walls. And best of all, it's downhill.

I found the guest house, an old shooting lodge called Talla Bheith, owned and run by Germans, mainly for Germans. Being told to dress for dinner from the contents of your saddlebag is rather challenging, but I didn't flinch as I selected my most tropical shirt. Going from the ridiculous bogs of Rannoch to the sublime splendour of the shooting lodge reminded me of *The Thirty-Nine Steps*. Dinner was a splendid affair and everyone switched from German to English to include me. This is an excellent place for lunch or a coffee stop if you are doing a circuit of Loch Rannoch.

Stage 3: Loch Rannoch-Braemar

I left Talla Bheith at 10.45. There was a following wind, which rustled the leaves and helped me along Loch Rannoch, where people were out fishing in little row boats. Kinloch Rannoch is the first real community after the loch, and has shops, hotels, B&Bs and a post office. I went and found the star of the bike scene, Jimmy White, who has a garage on the road south and stocks remarkably cheap second-hand bikes, as well as all sorts of spares. I oiled the chain and put on some new brake blocks while philosophizing on bicycle maintenance. I left town along the B846, which rolls through prosperous farmland and forestry, with beautiful birch woods. After 4 miles I took the B847 north. This bit of the route is hilly but you are rewarded with a breathtaking freewheel on quiet roads through Glen Errochty to Calvine, and on to Blair Atholl, enjoying the magnificent mature oaks.

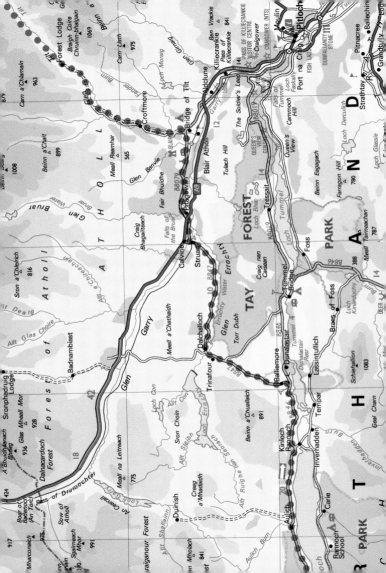

Blair Atholl is a curious little place, where everything is owned by the Duke of Atholl. All around is superb mountain bike country. The duke keeps the only private army in Europe so don't nick the artefacts if you visit the castle. (Admission charge.) There is a café in the Old Mill, and also a bike hire shop.

At 3.00, after a late lunch, I set off up Glen Tilt, heading along the south bank up a very steep hill, following the right of way signposted 'Braemar via Glen Tilt'.

Just before a farm the track turns into a grassy path which is a joy to cycle on, while on the other side of the stream a better Landrover track runs alongside. These come together about 2 miles further along. The track is excellent, sloping gently uphill, and is cycle-able to Belford Bridge, about 15 miles on. If you are sensible and stay on the right track, you leave the river valley after about 0.5 mile at the next burn and then head on a footpath north over the watershed for 1.5 miles, before rejoining a Landrover track after Loch Tilt.

Sadly, I managed to carry on along the river on a totally wrong route. I was in macho bash-on-with-it-and-it-will-come-right-mood, and when I couldn't even push my bike I manfully shouldered it and ploughed on. I am embarrassed to say that this folly continued for rather a long time, possibly hours. My water bottle fell off into the burn far below, which told me that the route had become impossibly steep.

The consequence of mountaineering with a bike happened in a rush. A handhold gave way and I fell about 15 ft. Fortunately I hit soft gravel and no damage was done. I started to get up, relieved, and then – wham – the bike landed on my head. Blood went everywhere and I waded into the river to wash. I completely panicked when I saw that the river had turned red. Staggering out, I wrapped my head in my shirt, and tried to get a grip on things. I was suffering from fairly serious blood loss. I didn't have a clue where I was. I found my compass and discovered I was heading due south when I thought I was going north.

For no reason I soldiered on for a bit, wading and towing my bike up the river like Humphrey Bogart with the *African Queen*. I was getting exhausted and weak so I did the first sensible thing in 2 hours and climbed out of the gorge and found a Landrover track after a couple of hundred yards. Never has a track been such a pleasant sight. It meant survival was likely.

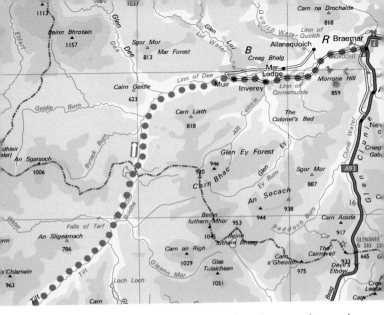

Even more relief came when I found myself at what turned out to be Fealach Lodge, where I was given a cup of tea and a sandwich by a keeper, who told me that the cut was just a superficial scratch. He put me on the right track and I left rather reluctantly at 8.30. I wandered up to a pole and crossed the deer-covered moor, then got onto the Landrover track I should have been on 3 hours before. At about 11 pm I arrived in Linn of Dee after roughly 14 miles. The track got progressively better, although there are some patches of loose gravel and sand which are a bit treacherous. In line with the bizarre nature of the day, the first cottage I found at Linn of Dee was selling honey so I went in. When they turned on a light and took a look I was sat down and kept talking.

From there everything was taken out of my control. I was given some tea and an ambulance was summoned. I spoke to a doctor and a policeman, and was loaded into an ambulance without my bike. I dozed on the stretcher fitfully, on the way to hospital in Aberdeen to be sewn up, and every time I opened my eyes I ruefully looked at the sign on the ambulance's ceiling saying 'Mind Your Head'.

GLASGOW, CLYDE COAST & EDINBURGH

Route maps are available free of charge from City of Glasgow Council and the Tourist Information Office in George Square, which show both the commuting and the leisure routes in the area. It is strongly recommended that visitors pick up updated leaflets, or have them sent by the Tourist Information Office. An advantage at the time of writing is that all Strathclyde Passenger Transport Executive trains permit bicycles free of charge on suburban services and trains to Ardrossan, Balloch, Gourock, Helensburgh, etc., subject to availability.

➤ **Glasgow-Balloch Cycle Path**
  ♦ Easy. 20 miles.

➤ **Glasgow-Paisley via the Renfrew Ferry**
  ♦ Easy. 10 miles.

➤ **Paisley-Greenock**
  ♦ Easy. 15 miles.

➤ **Paisley-Irvine**
  ♦ Easy. 25 miles.

➤ **Clyde Walkway from Glasgow Green to Uddingston**
  ♦ Easy, though best with a mountain bike in places. 8 miles.

➤ **Forth & Clyde Canal from Bowling through Glasgow to Falkirk**
  ♦ Easy. 36 miles.

➤ **Union Canal from Falkirk to Edinburgh**
  ♦ Easy, but care needed when crossing M9. 31 miles.

➤ **Water of Leith**
  ♦ Easy. 10 miles.

➤ **Some Common-sense Urban Cycling Tips**
  1. Make sure your bike is in perfect working order, particularly checking that the lights work.
  2. Choose a route that avoids the worst traffic congestion.
  3. Stop at traffic lights and try to act in a predictable way, so that motorists know you are there.
  4. Always obey the Highway Code.
  5. Don't drink and cycle.
  6. Leave your Walkman at home. You need to listen to be safe.
  7. Sue the local council if your bike gets damaged by potholes. See appendix for procedure.

Glasgow

• •

Unfortunately, Glasgow has a love affair with the car, and though it makes attempts at being more cyclist-friendly, these are generally rather half-hearted. Glasgow is quite hilly and has poor provision for cyclists. The result is that few people cycle in the city centre. If you want to campaign for better cycling facilities, contact Glasgow Cycling Campaign, 53 Cochrane Street, Glasgow G1. However, some cycle route maps can be obtained from the Tourist Information Office.

➤ OS Maps 63, 64, 65

➤ Tourist Information Office
11 George Square, tel. 0141 204-4400 (open all year)

➤ Cycle Shops
Glasgow has a full range of bike shops, from the plush, sleek showrooms to the equivalent of street stalls. There are also a fair number of bicycles changing hands in pubs. Please don't contribute to bike theft by buying buckshee bikes.
City centre
Bike Shop, 417 Alexandra Parade, tel. 0141 551-9393
Dales Cycles, 150 Dobies Loan, tel. 0141 332-2705
West End
Alan Hewitt, 500 Dumbarton Road, tel. 0141 339-0648
Allander Cycles, 3 South Mains Road, Milngavie, tel. 0141 956-6807
Bob Finnie, 1018 Maryhill Road, tel. 0141 945-1112. Archetypal cyclist rather than a businessman. Friendly service.
West End Cycles, 16 Chancellor Street, tel. 0141 357-1344
Gear, 19 Gibson Street, Hillhead, tel. 0141 339-1179
Out of town
These tend to be competitive price-wise and relaxed, and are worth checking out for larger purchases. It is also easier to try before you buy in places that hire bikes.
Wheelcraft, Unit 4, Aldessan House, Clachan of Campsie, tel. 01360 312709
Dooley's Cycles, 40 Moss Street, Paisley, tel. 0141 889-6090
Jim McMillan Cycles, 64 Sinclair Street, Helensburgh, tel. 01436 671915

➤ Hostels
SYHA, Glasgow, 7-8 Park Road, tel. 0141 332-3004. Newly opened in a former hotel. Continental breakfast and laundry facilities.
Glasgow Backpackers Hostel, Kelvin Lodge, 8 Park Circus, tel. 0141 332-5412. Real beds, not bunks, and no curfew.

Glasgow-Balloch Cycle Path

See Glasgow Fact Sheet

An excellent leaflet detailing this route, *The Glasgow Cycleway to Loch Lomond*, is available from Sustrans and is highly recommended. Beyond Balloch this route continues north and joins up with the area covered in Route 48. Eventually Sustrans intends to establish a route all the way to Inverness.

The route starts at Bell's Bridge, built over the Clyde at the time of the Glasgow Garden Festival in 1988. The route goes west from here on the north bank of the Clyde. Bell's Bridge is also the starting point for the cycle route from Glasgow to Paisley (see page 206).

The track is clearly signposted and follows the route of the Balloch railway service, allowing for an opt-out if necessary at a number of points along the way.

The Scottish Exhibition and Conference Centre is built on the site of former docks. The route passes the imposing Finnieston Crane, which was originally built for loading steam locomotives for export from Glasgow to the colonies. Cross the River Kelvin close to the Kelvin Hall in Glasgow's West End. The hall houses the interesting Museum of Transport, with early bicycles, as well as trams, fire engines, cars and ship models. (Free.) The river itself has gradually become less polluted following the decline of heavy industry and salmon and trout have returned.

Heading west, the route follows the Clyde Expressway and passes the sites of old shipyards which are now largely defunct. Crossing the Clyde is possible at the Clyde Tunnel, which has a cycle pathway. Further on at Yoker, the Renfrew Ferry allows foot and bicycle passengers to cross the river quite close to Glasgow Airport. From the ferry, with a bit of enterprise the Paisley to Greenock route (see page 207) can be joined.

At Clydebank the cycle track joins the Forth & Clyde Canal (see page 211). Clydebank Museum has displays describing the Roman occupation and the nearby Antonine Wall. It also details the shipbuilding history of Clydebank, where the great Cunard liners *Queen Mary*, *Queen Elizabeth* and the *QE2* were built at John Brown's Shipyard.

From Clydebank the route follows the canal to Bowling and then on to Dumbarton. There is a small bike shop at Bowling – Magic Cycles, tel. 01389 873433. There are lots of small boats here which are lovingly cared for, and the mooring has an eccentric charm.

Dumbarton is a reasonably sized town which is dominated by its castle, tel. 01389 32828, on a huge rocky outcrop overlooking the Clyde. The castle has been here since the 5thC, and much later Mary Queen of Scots took refuge here. (Admission charge.) The Denny Ship Model Experiment Tank is part of the Scottish Maritime Museum. (Admission charge.) The *Cutty Sark* was built by the Dumbarton shipbuilders Scott and Linton.

From Dumbarton the route heads up the River Leven to Balloch. Approaching Balloch is the site of the Balloch Radium Works, now the Riverside Boatyard, where a Scottish chemist, John Stewart Macarthur, reprocessed uranium and extracted radium. The early uses of radium are quite alarming. Radium fertilizer was used to produce monster carrots, and various quasi-medical applications such as radium mud baths were fashionable. In 1948 spoil from this site was inspected to see if it could be used in the nuclear weapons programme.

Balloch is a busy holiday town in summer and is on the southern banks of Loch Lomond. From here you can get the train back to Glasgow. Nearby is Loch Lomond SYHA hostel, tel. 01389 850226, off the A82 on the west side of the loch.

If you want to continue from Balloch and make a longer loop, head northwest along a minor road then the B834 and B818 via Croftamie to Fintry, and return over the Campsie Hills via the B822, known as the Crow Road, which rises to over 1000 ft. From Lennoxtown head southeast to the Forth & Clyde Canal at Lenzie, and follow the route on page 211 in reverse back to Glasgow.

Glasgow-Paisley via the Renfrew Ferry

See Glasgow Fact Sheet on page 204

A very good route map is available from Sustrans or from Tourist Information Offices. The route starts at Bell's Bridge and goes south-west through Govan, Bellahouston Park and along the White Cart

Water to Paisley Canal Station. Note that some parts of this route run through parks which are locked at night.

Bellahouston Park has the distinction of being used for an open-air Mass given by Pope John Paul II in 1982 and for being the location of Charles Rennie Mackintosh's recently realized House for an Art Lover. (Admission charge.) The route runs fairly close to Pollok Park, which houses the excellent Burrell Collection. (Free.)

Paisley is a town in its own right, with an identity distinct from Glasgow's. It is famous for its Paisley pattern shawls, and in the early 19thC the town dominated the British silk-spinning industry. The abbey, tel. 0141 889-7654, in the centre of Paisley, was founded by Walter Fitzalan, the steward of David I, c.1163 and is well worth a visit. It replaced the Celtic foundation of St Mirren, now the name of Paisley's football team. The St Mirren Chapel, dating from 1499, has a carved wall frieze depicting scenes from the life of the saint, an unusual survival in Protestant Scotland. Tearoom. (Free.) Another building of interest is the Coates Observatory, tel. 0141 889-2013, in the Oakshaw conservation area. The Coates were one of the wealthy spinning families and financed this observatory that has been recording astronomical and meteorological information since 1882.

Paisley-Greenock

See Glasgow Fact Sheet on page 204

Tourist Information Offices
Gourock, Station Road, tel. 01475 639467
Greenock, Municipal Buildings, Clyde Square, tel. 01475 724400
Paisley, Town Hall, Abbey Close, tel. 0141 889-0711 (summer only)

Excellent maps are available free from Sustrans, but broadly the route heads northwest via Bridge of Weir and Port Glasgow to Greenock. The route continues on from the Glasgow-Paisley route described above, and runs on former railway tracks. Various items of sculpture have been commissioned to add interest to the route. Quarriers Village was built as a children's home by William Quarrier in the late 19thC. Many of the stone villas are now privately owned and there's also a restaurant and craft centre.

From Greenock the route to Gourock follows the coast. The East India Docks are being developed. In 1987 the docks were seized by local boatowners who wanted to keep their boats here. The boats tended to be rickety and tarred together, and represented almost the last shipbuilding activity in the area. The owners claimed that the land had been bought in perpetuity by the people of Greenock in 1772 using a tax on beer. However, this argument didn't cut much ice with the Scottish courts and eventually the boats and their owners got chucked out. In Greenock the McLean Museum, tel. 01475 723741, in Kelly Street, has details on local industrial and social history, and there is an interesting collection of maritime paintings by Scottish Colourists. The architecture of Gourock and Greenock is solid, with many fine Victorian buildings along the waterfront.

You can of course head back to Glasgow by train. Alternatively, cross to Kilcreggan by Caledonian Macbrayne ferry and cycle on the B833 round to Helensburgh, where you can catch a train. A summer-only ferry operates to Helensburgh, enabling a quicker return to Glasgow along the north shore of the Clyde.

Paisley-Irvine

See Glasgow Fact Sheet on page 204

Tourist Information Offices
Ardrossan, Ferry Terminal, tel. 01294 601063 (summer only)
Irvine, New Street, tel. 01294 313886
Largs, The Promenade, tel. 01475 673765
Millport, 28 Stuart Street, tel. 01475 530735 (summer only)
Paisley, Town Hall, Abbey Close, tel. 0141 889-0711 (summer only)

The Sustrans leaflet for this route from Paisley to Irvine and Ardrossan has an excellent map.

The route largely follows disused railway tracks, leaving Paisley Canal station for Johnstone, Castle Semple Loch, Beith, Kilwinning and Irvine. Here it connects with the Grand Tour (see Route 1).

The route passes Kilbarchan close to the National Trust's Weaver's Cottage, tel. 01505 705588, which dates from 1723 and houses the last of the village's looms. (Admission charge.) Further along is Castle Semple Country Park, a popular centre for watersports, tel. 01505 842882. There is an RSPB nature reserve at the south end of the loch. (Free.)

Near Dalry is Dalgarven Mill, tel. 01294 552448, a 17thC watermill whose granaries have been converted into exhibition galleries with artefacts of social and agricultural interest, as well as a collection of doll's houses.

Just past Kilwinning is a branch west to Eglinton Country Park, with 1000 acres of wooded parkland. You can visit the remains of Eglinton Castle, now a ruin and the site of a great jousting tournament in 1839, aimed at reliving the Age of Chivalry. Unfortunately it was beaten by the inclement Scottish weather. Now there is a visitor centre and nature trails, and jousting is definitely frowned on.

In Irvine the Scottish Maritime Museum, tel. 01294 278283, has an excellent collection of vessels, from fishing boats to lifeboats, and also has the world's oldest tea clipper, the *Carrick*. (Admission charge.)

Clyde Walkway
from Glasgow Green to Uddingston

See Glasgow Fact Sheet on page 204

◆

The route starts at the Scottish Exhibition and Conference Centre in the heart of Glasgow. It goes east from Bell's Bridge, and as long as you keep the Clyde to your right you are doing OK. There is a partial walkway and a road that continues east past the St Enoch Centre. To stick by the river you have to get onto the pavement and walk for a block, because of the one-way system. Opposite the High Court Buildings are the gates to Glasgow Green.

Glasgow Green has a rich history, which is well-covered at the People's Palace, Glasgow's social history museum, which includes, among other things, Billy Connolly's Banana Feet shoes. (Free.) The Green is part of Glasgow's ancient common lands, dating in its present form from 1792 when the last piece, Flesher's Haugh, was added. This area is where Bonnie Prince Charlie's troops paraded in 1746, though Glasgow did not give the Jacobites much help. The park was created in the early 19thC, although people continued to wash clothes and graze cattle and sheep here into the 20thC.

The Green is perhaps best known as the focus of social unrest and popular protest, from the Carlton weavers in 1787, to the Red Clydesiders and the Poll Tax and Criminal Justice Bill demonstrations more recently. It also has some fine sculptures, including the Maclennan Arch and the Doulton Fountain (now, sadly, inoperative), and the huge Nelson Monument. The Green is a jealously guarded public space, which always seems under threat of development of one sort or another.

The Clyde and its banks are used for a variety of sports, including running and cycling, and also rowing. Going through the Green you pass the Glasgow Humane Society boathouse, and the house lived in by George Parsonage. He has continued the work of his father, rescuing people from the Clyde, as well as recovering bodies. Continue across King's Drive into the area of the park used by footballers, known as Flesher's Haugh.

From the Green onwards the route gets quite isolated and is sparsely used. I feel that I should warn cyclists that this part of Glasgow is quite rough and visitors should be wary, as it is possible to encounter aggression, and women should be careful, especially if they are on their own. It is advisable to avoid the area after dark.

The route continues on the north bank, past Celtic Football Club's brand-new Parkhead stadium and Belvedere Hospital to Carmyle.

Just after Carmyle cross the Clyde on a magnificent disused viaduct and then proceed on the south bank in attractive countryside until the walkway comes to the Rotten Calder Burn, so-called because of the iron which makes it flow a rust red. Cutting upriver there is a footbridge across the burn and then under the railway. The route then cuts across Blantyre Farm Road and into the newly-established Calder Glen Country Park before continuing to another bridge over the Clyde. From here it is worthwhile continuing upriver to Bothwell Castle, a red sandstone ruin and one of the grandest in Scotland. It was built in the 13thC for Walter of Morovia and besieged on a number of occasions. It is now in the care of Historic Scotland. (Admission charge.) Continue to Uddingston and return by train to Glasgow.

Forth & Clyde Canal
from Bowling through Glasgow to Falkirk

See Glasgow Fact Sheet on page 204

♦

Tourist Information Office
Falkirk, 2 Glebe Street, tel. 01324 620244

Cycle Shops
City Cycles, 48 Vicar Street, Falkirk, tel. 01324 613302
G.W. Smith, High Street, Falkirk, tel. 01324 621227
Pedal Power Cycles, 51 West End, West Calder, tel. 01506 873123

This route links with that described on page 204

There is an excellent map and information pack available from British
Waterways, Canal House, 1 Applecross Street, Glasgow G4 9SP, tel.
0141 332-6936.

The Forth & Clyde Canal opened in 1790 and one of its major
features is a 400 ft aqueduct across the River Kelvin. The canal was
abandoned in 1962 because of falling demand, and partly destroyed
by roadbuilding projects. However, there has been a substantial
effort put into restoring the canal for leisure use, and a 12 mile
section is now reopened.

The route between Bowling and Maryhill in northwest Glasgow is
breached in several places and is hard to follow, so the junction near
Lochburn Road, north of Maryhill Road is probably the best point to
start. From Maryhill Road go along Lochburn Road and pass under
the viaduct to join the path that proceeds east. This is close to the
Kelvin Aqueduct, 0.5 mile west and worth visiting.

The track varies considerably in quality according to the area it passes through, but it is cycle-able all the way. There are many other
users of the canal towpath, including walkers and anglers. The canal
is a haven for wildlife of various sorts. At Lenzie the canal runs close
to the remains of the Antonine Wall, which continues to Falkirk. This
was a defensive structure built by the Romans c.AD 139, and abandoned in AD 155, in an attempt to control the lowland Scots. Unlike
Hadrian's Wall, it was built largely of turf. Various forts have been

identified along the route. The best remains may be seen around Falkirk, including at Rough Castle, 6 miles west of Falkirk on the B816, where there are ramparts and ditches. (Free.)

At Falkirk, cross the town to join the Union Canal route. See the detailed map supplied by the British Waterways Board.

Union Canal from Falkirk to Edinburgh

See Edinburgh Fact Sheet

Tourist Information Office
Linlithgow, Burgh Halls, The Cross, tel. 01506 844600

For more details, contact the British Waterways Board.

The major hazard on this route is the fact that beyond Falkirk it is cut by the M9. The British Waterways Board map shows this. However, if you come to the motorway, do not attempt to cross it. Backtrack and turn left, crossing the M9 via a little road which passes under the motorway and also a railway bridge. Then turn left again and follow the road until it rejoins the canal. From here continue east past Ratho and into the outskirts of Edinburgh at Sighthill.

Linlithgow has various attractions to recommend it. Linlithgow Palace, tel. 0131 244-3101, is a splendid ruin next to the loch. The chapel and hall are late 15thC and there is an ornate 16thC fountain. Mary Queen of Scots was born here, and in 1746 the building was accidentally burnt by Hanoverian troops. (Admission charge.)

The canal passes the Linlithgow Union Canal Society Museum, which also does cruises. Housed in the former stables for the canal horses, this is a must for people interested in the history of the Union Canal, which was opened in 1822. It is free to enter, although the cruises have a charge, and there is also a tearoom. Another site of interest is Niddry Castle, tel. 01506 890753, dating from the 15thC and yet another refuge for Mary Queen of Scots.

At Ratho, 8 miles out of Edinburgh, is the Edinburgh Canal Centre, tel. 0131 333-1320/1251, which also does canal cruises, and has a bar with outdoor seating, as well as exhibitions on the canal and canal life.

Edinburgh

Edinburgh is blessed with a number of cycle tracks and these are well explained in leaflets with good maps available from City of Edinburgh Council, Highways Department, 19 Market Street, Edinburgh EH1 1BL. Send an SAE. Also pick up Spokes Cycling Campaign leaflets, available from cycle shops in the city. Spokes is Edinburgh's cycle campaign (St Martin's Church, 232 Dalry Road, tel. 0131 313-2114) and issues very good maps with the routes clearly marked. These are highly recommended if you are spending much time in Edinburgh. Bike theft is rife in Edinburgh, so look after your possessions. And Edinburgh has a lot of cobbled streets which rattle the teeth but do wonders for cellulite! Cycling in big cities always seems fraught with difficulty and Edinburgh is no different – its hills are killers.

➤ OS Maps 66, 67

➤ **Tourist Information Office**
3 Princes Street, tel. 0131 557-2727 (open all year)

➤ **Cycle Shops**
Edinburgh is liberally sprinkled with shops dealing in bike hire, spares and repairs.
Edinburgh Bicycles, 5-8 Alvanley Terrace, off Brunswick Place, tel. 0131 228-1368
Central Cycle Hire, The New Bike Shop and The Bicycle Repair Shop, all at 13 Lochrin Place, near Tollcross, tel. 0131 228-6333/ 6633
Jocky Allan Cycles, 115 Leith Walk, tel. 0131 554-6698
Clan Cycles, 151 Buccleuch Street, tel. 0131 668-4144
Bargain Bikes, 151 Buccleuch Street, tel. 0131 668-4144
City Cycles, 30 Rodney Street, tel. 0131 557-2801
Freewheelin', 91 Slateford Road, tel. 0131 337-2351
Williamson, 26 Hamilton Place, tel. 0131 225-3286
Cycles, 12 West Preston Street, tel. 0131 667-6239

➤ **Hostels**
SYHA, Eglington, 18 Eglington Crescent, tel. 0131 337-1120
SYHA, Bruntsfield, 7 Bruntsfield Crescent, tel. 0131 447-2994
High Street Hostel, 8 Blackfriars Street, tel. 0131 557-3984

Additional excursions to those described here are outlined in Chapter 9: The Borders.

Water of Leith

◆ See Edinburgh Fact Sheet on page 213

The Water of Leith rises in the Pentland Hills and is the best that Edinburgh can do in terms of a river. It is really rather lovely, considering it acted as the city's main sewer for a couple of centuries. Paradoxically, it now teems with wildlife, including badgers, and is reputed to contain trout. The route starts at Balerno, and follows the river to Leith. Equally, in reverse it is a useful off-road route out of the city. From Balerno you are well placed to explore the Pentland Hills.

If you are starting in Edinburgh itself, join the route at the west end of Prince's Street in the city centre and continue to Dean Village along Queensferry Road, where a steep hill goes down to the left. You emerge in a leafy valley with neoclassical statues, which is a remarkable oasis 2 minutes from the bustle of Princes Street.

Now basically follow the river down to Leith. It is a bit complicated, but you should keep your eye on the river, crossing and re-crossing it several times. The route goes through a very interesting cross-section of Edinburgh. Dean Village is distinctly posh, and has a sculpture or two to prove it, while at Stockbridge you cross the river and go along Arboretum Avenue past the Royal Botanic Garden, which has a good tearoom.

Pass the inevitable crematorium and football stadium, which are the staple of urban cycle tracks, and carry on through Bonnington before emerging at Leith, where there are various eating places. It is quite a short route but it is rather special and provides a completely different perspective of Edinburgh.

Other short routes in Edinburgh are discussed in Chapter 9 and further short sections of cycle track are best tackled with the Spokes Map, which is widely available in Edinburgh. Mountain bikes are often used on the Pentland Hills south of Edinburgh, using tracks marked on OS maps. However, these have become overused and restrictions have now been imposed by the Pentland Park Authority.

PLANNING YOUR CYCLING HOLIDAY

Preparation is extremely important if you're going to have an enjoyable cycling holiday. Nothing spoils a holiday for you, and for your travelling companions, so much as sitting in a roadside ditch miles from anywhere without the tools to repair a bike. Generally bikes are remarkably robust, provided they are oiled and the tyres pumped up, and are not ludicrously overloaded. Other things like brake blocks and cables should be checked. If in doubt or if you can't be bothered, do get a bike shop to check over your bike before you set out. A good test of whether your bike works properly is to go out for a short cycle ride prior to your holiday.

Checking your bike

The type of bike is much less important than the marketing gurus would like you to think, and an old boneshaker of the sort that made the Empire great will get you to much the same places as the sleekest racer or the knobbliest mountain bike.

Here is a quick guide to bike maintenance. First check that your bike is carefully dusted and free of bat droppings, then check for broken, loose or worn parts, particularly broken or loose spokes, and check that your wheels are not buckled. Also check for worn tyres; often the sidewall gets damaged if the bicycle is used when the tyres are flat or the bike is excessively loaded. Tyres have to be pumped very hard. Do not believe people who tell you that the compressors at garages will be unable to blow your tyres up to full pressure. I had a humbling experience when I pumped up my tyres rock-hard with a line and both burst with amazing sound effects as I got on, to the amusement of a young woman in a rather nice sports car who was using the car wash! The tyres state the pressure as usually 45 psi for mountain bikes, and 70-80 psi for road bikes.

Make sure your bike is set up right. One of the most common mistakes is having the saddle too low. This is particularly a problem on mountain bikes, because the pedal cranks are set high to provide extra ground clearance. This means that you can probably barely touch the ground from the saddle, and crossbars seem designed to punish mistakes. To check that the saddle height is correct, sit on the saddle with your heel on the pedal at its lowest cranking position. Your leg should be almost straight, but not in a 'locked' position. When riding, place the ball of your foot on the pedal.

Listen to what your body is saying as you cycle along and try to adjust your position to suit. Knees can suffer because of the saddle being too low or because too high a gear has been selected. Touring bikes with drop handlebars give a greater range of ride positions which prevent you from seizing up too much. Mountain bikes can be fitted with bar ends for much the same reason. Wearing a rucksack while cycling is bad news and can damage your back and wrists.

Saddles are very personal. Many people are convinced by gel saddles, which seem pretty good. However, it all depends on your bone structure, and you should experiment until you find one that suits you. Other old-timers swear by leather saddles. In practice, all types of saddle seem to be a bit uncomfortable until you are fit. Generally, narrow saddles are used on racing bikes and wider saddles on more conventional, sit-up-and-beg bikes.

What to take

This depends on how long you are going for and where you are going to stay. If you are going to camp, it means carrying large and heavy loads. Many people follow this course of action, but it certainly detracts from the enjoyment of cycling, and increases the odds of overloading the bike. Under no circumstances should you carry belongings in a rucksack, as this will hurt your back.

However, camping offers a freedom and a cheapness which compensate for the times when you feel like a yak or some other less glamorous beast of burden. It is worth noting that compared to walking with a heavy pack, cycling with loaded panniers is a cinch. On the other hand, if you are staying at youth hostels, bothies, independent hostels, hotels or B&Bs, and are intending to eat out, you should be able to survive by leaving your panniers at home, and using a saddle bag instead.

Packing

Belongings should be put in plastic bags to keep them dry, and bags placed in panniers or saddlebags. Make sure all bags are firmly secured to the bike rack. Most people carry far too much on their bikes. If you have a wonderful set of panniers with 20 litres' volume you will carry 21 litres-worth of belongings. If you take a 5 litre saddle bag, you will take 6 litres-worth.

Packing a saddle bag is closely akin to striving for the Buddhist state of nirvana. Both are a quest for detachment from earthly possessions, and attaining nirvana is probably easier. After much practice my technique is as follows. I put out everything I want to take. Then I remove the spare jumpers, underwear, books, cooker and chopsticks and end up with the bare minimum. It is quite possible to survive with a saddle bag containing some compact spare clothes, bike tools, a camera and enough food and water, and the compensations of travelling light do outweigh the benefits of lugging the stuff around. By and large you can drink water from burns in the Scottish Highlands provided that there are no houses or roads upstream and a reasonable volume of water is flowing. The normal advice for cyclists, especially in hot conditions, is to drink little and often.

Clothes

Most people wear a light, Gore-Tex-style outer jacket, usually with a T-shirt and maybe a shirt. Rather than carrying one warm sweater, it is much better to carry several thin layers so you can control body temperature. Cotton, wool and silk are good as you can go for days and they don't get too rancid. For compactness and speed of drying, Rohan-style trousers are great, and also have secure pockets. I wear woolly socks for the reason that your feet and other extremities get cold. Even in summer, good gloves and a hat are essential. As footwear I wear a pair of standard cross trainers. I like to be able to get off and walk, and the specialist cycling shoes with metal bases are too specialized for me. Instead I use old-fashioned toe clips with leather straps. However, specialist shoes which lock onto the pedals are arguably better than pedals with toe clips if you crash. They have quick-release mechanisms like ski binding. Stiffer-soled shoes are more efficient and less stressful on the feet. NOTE: It is virtually impossible to walk with metal studs on your feet.

You will encounter all manner of specialized cycling clothes on a visit to any bike shop. Fashionable materials are bright Lycra and some of the more unholy chamois fabrics, but these are being replaced by garments crammed full of antibacterial agents to stop crotch rot and even nastier lifeforms from emerging. Fortunately a few manufacturers are starting to market less garish clothes which look reasonable, so you could actually go into a pub without everyone giggling and pointing. Gore-Tex and similar fabrics are amazingly effective waterproof fabrics. They are expensive but if you've got the money it is a sound investment. Nothing spoils cycling holidays more than getting wet. The special cycling Gore-Tex tops are incredibly light, but rip very easily if you fall off, and also seem surprisingly expensive. Gore-Tex clothes suitable for walking and running are cheaper and more resilient, and are worth looking at before you buy.

For winter cycling there are neoprene tops which prevent you from getting too cold even when you are wet. The actual garment is not so crucial, but the emergence of light waterproofs that are really waterproof is an advantage which has transformed cycling in Scotland.

Safety considerations

There are few natural hazards facing the intrepid cyclist, although it is possible to get chased by cows or swooped on by nesting birds. The unnatural hazards of course are cars and lorries, which you get everywhere, but they do tend to be repelled by bright colours. Bike lights are useful, but are more effective out of town where there are no street lights. Reflectors are also very effective. It is worth noting that the two worst times for traffic in rural Scotland are about 5 pm, when commuters are going home, and after 11 pm, when the pubs shut. Of course, if you are cycling at 11 at night you are probably on the way back from the pub too.

First aid

It sometimes seems hard to believe but sunburn in Scotland is a serious hazard, mainly because you are not expecting it and because the air temperature is not high. Scottish summer days are very long, with sunrise at 5 am and sunset as late as 11 pm. There is a lot of time to get sunburnt in between. Sun cream is essential, preferably waterproof, as you will sweat it off. Sunglasses are also essential, not only when it is sunny, but also when there are insects around. Ozone depletion has meant that ultraviolet radiation is no longer filtered naturally. This radiation is a serious health risk. The wrong sort of sunglasses can actually cause your eyes to dilate, and allow in more damaging radiation. It is important that sunglasses state they protect against UVa and UVb radiation. Make sure they are unbreakable.

A small first-aid kit is useful, containing plasters, midge repellent, and lip and skin cream. Your face does dry up and crack in the wind. Generally though, survival equipment needed for hillwalking is unnecessary on bikes, although this of course depends on where you are going.

Helmets

Opinions vary hugely on whether or not helmets are worth wearing. They do provide some protection, but to my mind seriously detract from the enjoyment of the ride. There is some evidence that helmets encourage people to take more risks because they feel protected.

Food

Food is absolutely essential on bikes. Dried fruit like apricots, dates, nuts and raisins, as well as chocolate bars and sandwiches, are all great. Cycling is a demanding physical activity and you can suffer a condition in which your blood sugar levels fall (called 'bonk' by old-time cyclists). It is unpleasant and you get rubbery legs, but an input of energy in the form of biscuits and sandwiches is a remarkable instant cure. It is a crime against humanity to cycle past any available café, and 'drumming up' cups of tea over stoves is a very therapeutic activity as well.

Planning – but not overplanning – your trip

It is a bit worrying advising people on how to plan a trip when the advice might be, 'Don't do it'. You go places to see things and not just to cycle. If you just want to clock up miles you could sit on an exercise bike. You have to be honest about your capabilities. Most people can manage to cycle 20-30 miles per day. Others could easily do 120 miles. Start with shorter distances and gradually work your way up. After a few days it is not hard to do 80-90 miles in a day, particularly during the Scottish summer when the days are very long. You just keep going for longer and take big breaks.

Tourists doing the Grand Tour described in this book should know that doing long distances day after day does get wearing and you are likely to get niggling injuries. It is much more fun to stay with sensible distances most of the time, but have some long days as well as some rest days. Remember that touring is a holiday – if you find a nice stream to sit by or a beautiful birch wood, do enjoy them. And if you are in a group, remember that you will, like it or not, have to go at the pace of the slowest.

When is the best time?

You can cycle at any time, and it can be extremely rewarding, even in winter. But the best time of year in Scotland is probably spring and early summer. April, May and June always seem stunning, with the exception of bank holidays. You get settled sunny weather, the trees bursting into leaf and the wild flowers coming out. Later in the summer the airstream gets wetter. The most convincing explanation is that the air passing over the Atlantic Ocean picks up more moisture as summer progresses, so there is more water to fall out over the west of Scotland when it gets there. Eastern Scotland does tend to be considerably drier but a bit cooler. While the rain in the west of Scotland can be tiresome, it is the reason for the vibrant green foliage which makes this part of the country so special. If you are travelling out of season, i.e. October-Easter, you will find that many services are reduced, and B&Bs close down. Careful planning is then required and it is essential to telephone ahead and check things out. It is also vital that your bike has reflectors and working lights.

Accommodation

Deciding where to stay is a relatively simple matter, but it is of crucial importance to the enjoyment and cost of your holiday. It is possible to book in advance using Tourist Information Offices, but it is often possible to negotiate lower prices in person, and you sometimes find places that you like just by stumbling on them.

Hotels

In Scotland hotels seem like the first choice, if you can afford them, although their quality levels are mixed. I like small village hotels which are the focus of the community and tend to be quite cheap, i.e. £20 per night. However, some have hushed dining rooms and can be lonely places. Smaller hotels with good pubs are worth seeking out since they are great experiences. With luck you can unearth some folk music and a 'lock-in' at the bar, which can develop into an enjoyable evening.

Bed and Breakfast (B&B)

The characteristically British form of accommodation is the bed and breakfast, which is wonderful for people like me who love being nosy and looking at other people's houses. Again, the standards vary enormously but basically you are going into a normal person's house and often using their children's unused bedrooms. They are cheaper than hotels, although not that cheap, ranging from £12-18 per night. Generally, they are friendly places and the breakfasts are generous.

Youth Hostels

These are a very useful – in fact, a near-vital – facility for cycle touring on a budget. The Scottish Youth Hostels Association (SYHA) is a membership organization which you have to join before staying anywhere, although you can pay your £6 fee at most hostels. The advantages are very considerable. Hostels are cheap (around £4-7 per night) self-catering. You are also required to use an approved sleeping sheet, or to pay 60p to hire one. Since many hostel sleeping sheets are now of nylon, you not only get sweaty and cannot sleep, but also run the risk of being electrocuted when you get up due to the static build-up. In other words, it may be worth bringing your own cotton sleeping sheet. Sleeping bags are usually banned, except in some remote hostels. Be warned: the warden has the power, although probably not the inclination, to inspect your bedding.

Hostels do have their drawbacks, though. If you are going to use them you really have to be in on time and be prepared to live with rules and regulations, such as the strict curfew times, which admittedly are not everyone's cup of tea. Sometimes wardens seem officious but the more remote hostels tend to be friendlier.

Independent Hostels

These are very varied and are part of a rapidly expanding network. They tend to have good self-catering facilities, and cater more for 'real travellers', such as footloose Australians. There are thirty hostels on the mainland, and various others on the islands. Some are more luxurious than others, and cost £3-10 per night. At some you will need a sleeping bag, although usually if you don't have one you will manage somehow. There is no curfew and no rules, except those that govern the bulk of humanity. The various hostels I have used are very friendly, and I strongly welcome the emergence of this network and hope it continues to grow.

Camping

Basically, the rule is 'Don't do it'. You get laden down like a yak, which is no fun. But it is undoubtedly a wonderful thing to wake up in a tent next to the sea on a crisp sunny morning and to be able to go swimming before breakfast.

Camping Facilities

Camp sites are liberally scattered throughout Scotland and details of them are available at Tourist Information Offices. They tend to have showers and toilet blocks, and grass to put your tent on. Alternatively, in the wilder parts of Scotland, like Glen Affric or Knoydart, you can generally camp in any sensible place, but if necessary do get the landowner's permission first. Pubs are usually quite happy for you to camp nearby and may also let you use showers and the facilities. Often, nomad villages develop around particularly obliging hostelries.

Camping Barns

These are bare, waterproof buildings with Spartan facilities, and are good if it's chucking it down with rain, at least if you have camping gear. They don't have kitchens or much in the way of facilities, but are quite cheap. In the Western Isles barns are known as Gatcliff Trust Hostels, while on Shetland there is a useful network of Bods. Camping barns are a new development and a helpful addition to the available options.

Bothies

There is a wide network of bothies all over Scotland, which are rather like unofficial camping barns. They are open buildings, in the sense that they are unlocked and available free of charge for genuine travellers. They are maintained by various people, but the Mountain Bothies Association looks after many of them with volunteer help. Facilities are variable, and tend to get run down and vandalized, which is tragic. Because of this the Mountain Bothies Association is against publicizing the whereabouts of bothies except to people who take the trouble to find out. However, if you are intending to explore off the beaten track in Scotland, send your £10 cheque to join the Mountain Bothies Association, which will provide a list of bothies and other vital information. Contact Ted Butcher at 26 Rycroft Avenue, Deeping St Jades, Peterborough PE6 8NT, tel. 01778 345062.

Sleeping out

This is something which remarkably few people try, but in fine weather it is a serious alternative to camping and is a great experience, so why not give it a go? Modern Gore-Tex bivvy bags are brilliant, but even without one you can sleep in a sleeping bag on a reasonably warm night.

Try to find a dry patch of ground and be a bit cautious about where you sleep. Camping on the beach is fine but remember about tides. One friend's attempt at sleeping out ended when he woke up to hear a slopping noise, and found he was drifting out to sea, supported by his remarkable Gore-Tex sleeping bag.

How to get there

The choices obviously depend on where you are starting from and where you are going to. The most useful transport for cyclists has always been the train, but changes to the UK's railways have been making life harder for cyclists and it is clear that they are not really interested in carrying bikes. The reasons are baffling, but that is another issue. Trains will still take bikes for a set booking fee of £3, which is OK for long journeys but has made short hops prohibitively expensive. Bookings can be made at staffed BR stations, and Edinburgh has a telesales office, tel. 0131 556-2451. The drawback here is that you can only book above a value of £10 with a credit card. Another alternative is Rail Direct, based in Newcastle, tel. 0800 450450, which is a freephone telesales number. However, they prefer to send tickets to the card-holder's home address, which isn't too handy if you live in Germany or if you are already on holiday in a remote part of the Highlands. Using trains is best if you book in advance and stick to your planned timetable.

In summer there is vastly more demand for bike space than is provided, and booking bikes on trains tends to be difficult, especially by phone. Trains on the West Coast, like the ferries, do not run on the Sabbath. Buses have tightened up on the carriage of bicycles, and provision is hit or miss. In many rural areas it is possible informally to take a bike on buses, but it depends on available space.

Carrying bikes by car

Sadly, the car is virtually the only option for the transportation of bicycles to many starting points. Mountain biking is based on the assumption that you will get there by car. Roof racks are hard to load but have the advantage of getting the bikes clear of lights and numberplates. Rear cycle carriers are extremely easy to use. However, the police get unhappy if the carrier blocks the licence plate, so some people fit a tail board as well.

Rear cycle carriers are better aerodynamically. Of course, you should remember to remove anything like bicycle pumps, which can fall off, or which other people might remove. And if you are going to leave the bike on the car, take quick-release wheels and saddles off. One problem with bike racks which has emerged is that some people hang the bikes too near to the exhaust, and the tyres get damaged.

Hiring a bike

Most hire bikes are mountain bikes, because they are fairly robust. It is virtually impossible to hire real road bikes. Hire rates seem inordinately expensive, with a typical bike costing £10-15 per day. If you consider a couple hiring two bikes, it can cost more more than it does to hire a car for the day. Note that hire companies have limited seasons.

Organized tours

Think carefully before booking accommodation in advance, because of being too organized. However, if you like to be organized, and prefer to have the trip organized on your behalf, there are various organizations specializing in bespoke cycling holidays which will book your accommodation, ferries and rail tickets, and provide you with a suitable bike. Some will even carry your luggage and give you a mobile telephone, which is really decadent.

Bespoke Highland Tours concentrate on the West of Scotland and the islands. Ian Pragnell, the man at the helm, is an enthusiastic cyclist, and produces meticulously planned routes customized to the needs of the customer. He provides maps and bikes, although you can use your own.
Bespoke Highland Tours, The Bothy, Camusdarach by Arisaig, Inverness-shire, tel. 0141 334-9017 or 01687 450272.

Roundabout Scotland has group tours in Dumfries and Galloway, Islay and Arran, and Speyside.
Roundabout, 4 Observatory Lane, Glasgow G12 9AH, tel. 0141 337-3877.

The Scottish Youth Hostels Association organizes guided cycling holidays to the Western Isles. They are quite sociable and well priced but you can easily overdose on hostels.
SYHA National Office, 7 Glebe Crescent, Stirling, tel. 01786 451181.

Bikebus organizees some sociable weekend tours leaving from Edinburgh, and longer holidays too.
4 Barclay Terrace, Edinburgh EH10 4HP, tel. 0131 229-6274.

Mountains and Glens organizes fixed-base holidays at Blairgowrie with a series of day trips. Guides are an optional extra.
Railway Road, Welton Industrial Estate, Blairgowrie, tel. 01250 874206.

Scottish Cycling Holidays provides routes mainly in the eastern and central parts of Scotland, which seem remarkably good value. Surprisingly, the company stipulates that the combined weight of cyclist and luggage must not exceed 14 stones.
Ballintruim Post Office, Blairgowrie, Perthshire, tel. 01250 886201.

How much does it cost?

Cycling in Scotland is not particularly cheap. The cost of ferries, trains and B&Bs, as well as eating out, soon mounts up. The organized tours listed on the previous page cost (at 1996 prices) roughly £150 for a hostel tour or £350 per week for travel, B&B and bike hire, although this can go much higher depending on service. If you book accommodation personally, a similar cost to those for organized tours would be reasonable. In addition, there is the cost of eating lunch and evening meals and snacks, which adds about £10 per day. Self-catering at hostels is obviously cheaper.

Weather

Although this is important, there is not much point in worrying about it, except on the hills. Weather Line numbers cost 50p per min, 40p per min off-peak. A forecast will cost about £3.

Highlands	0891 500425
Aberdeen	0891 500424
Perthshire	0891 500423
Edinburgh	0891 500422
West Scotland	0891 500421
Dumfries and Galloway	0891 500420
Mountain Line	
West Scotland	0891 500441
East Scotland	0891 500442

Alternatively, you could do your own basic weather forecasting. Really heavy showers are usually preceded by a rush of air, so a gust of wind is a warning that it's time to don your waterproofs. At normal temperatures, rhododendron leaves are upright and horizontal. As soon as the temperature drops near freezing they start to droop, so beware of ice on the track. Hens are sensible and get indoors before the rain starts. Sheep and cattle also take shelter before rain or snow, and sheep come down off the tops when snow is imminent.

Breakdowns

If you are really keen to be secure, join the Environmental Transport Association, Old Post House, Heath Road, Weybridge, Surrey KT13 7RS, tel. 01932 828882, which runs an insurance and a breakdown and rescue service similar to the AA or RAC, but which covers both cars and bikes. People joining the ETA can sign up to a cycle service which promises to get you to a bike shop or railway station from wherever your bike disintegrates, although they don't mend punctures! In contrast to the RAC and AA, this organization campaigns actively for an integrated transport policy, which includes cycling and public transport, and deserves to be supported.

In addition to the essential services listed above, local Tourist Information Offices will also be able to provide extra information. Their addresses are given in the fact sheets which appear throughout this book.

An alternative and useful service is Talking Pages, tel. 0800 600900, a freephone number which lists all sorts of services free of charge.

Accidents

Try not to have accidents, or to get lost. I am firmly of the opinion that accidents don't happen unless people let them happen. The concern about cycle helmets is that people do stupid things because they feel safe wearing them. I don't know any relevant research on cyclists, but some people wearing seat belts feel invulnerable and drive more aggressively. If you plan to get lost, take survival gear, some flares and a good book.

What to do if you have an accident.
1. Keep calm, and keep your temper.
2. Note down the registration number of the vehicle involved immediately.
3. If there are no independent witnesses call the police immediately, but first tell the driver you are doing so.

4. Get the names and addresses of any witnesses. Without independent witnesses you will find it harder to win in court.

5. Get the driver's name and address, and insurance company name.

6. Note any damage to you, your bicycle and other vehicles.

7. Draw a map of the location with measurements if possible, and details of traffic signs. Note the time and the weather. This can all be very useful in court.

8. Do not admit blame or say sorry, even if you think the accident was your fault. It may jeopardize your insurance claim.

9. Report the accident to the police. This is very important, even if you are not injured. If the driver is convicted of drunken, dangerous or careless driving, it will improve your chance of getting compensation. Press for charges to be brought in such a case.

The highways department decides where to install safety features depending on how many reported accidents there are. The more reported accidents, the stronger the case for special cycle facilities.

Remember it is an offence to open a vehicle door so as to injure any person. This means a driver could be convicted even if his door causes a cyclist to swerve.

It is an offence to leave a vehicle on a road in such a position as to cause danger to other people using the road. Note the number of any parked cars which may have contributed to the accident.

Pothole claim procedure

This advice is intended to be helpful, but no responsibility can be accepted for any inaccuracies, problems or losses arising from its use. One way of persuading council highways departments to ensure that roads are safe for cycling, and indeed walking or driving, on is by telling them, and getting them to act on potholes before you have an accident or damage your bike. However, if substandard road surfacing does damage your cycle or cause serious injury to a rider, you can claim compensation from the local authority, which has a legal responsibility to ensure that its roads are maintained in a safe condition.

Who will handle the claim?

1. If you are a member of the Cyclist Touring Club you will have access to its free legal assistance scheme and should contact the club as soon as possible.

2. Your trade union may have a free legal-aid scheme which could assist you.

3. If your claim is below £750, you could handle the claim yourself through the small claim procedure, at a sheriff or magistrates court. Under this procedure, even if you lose, no expenses can be awarded against you if the claim is under £200, and a maximum of £75 if your claim is between £200 and £750. Citizens' advice bureaux give details of the exact procedure, and leaflets are available at sheriff and magistrates courts.

4. For more serious injuries, you may wish to employ a solicitor, but lawyers' fees are considerable.

What information should you have to make your claim more likely to succeed?

However your claim is handled, you should try to get the following information as soon as possible after the accident.

1. Name and address of the local highways department.

2. Name of the road and town where the incident occurred, and the nearest building or number.

3. The position of the hole in the road, i.e. northbound or southbound, and distance from the kerb.

4. Date and time of the incident.

5. Names and addresses of eyewitnesses or of any cyclists who use the route regularly and can testify to the existence of the defect. At the time of the incident, or as soon as possible afterwards, prop up your bike and photograph it with one wheel in the hole or broken road surface as evidence of the size of the defect and how it interacts with the cycle wheel. Also take a photo with a ruler held vertically in the pothole.

6. Description of any injuries, however minor. Note that if you are claiming in court, the law allows you to prove it with the evidence of one witness, i.e. yourself, if there has been personal injury. Under the small claims procedure only one witness is required but if there is only damage to property more than one witness is needed. In all cases a report from your doctor or

hospital prepared as soon as possible after the incident will not only corroborate your story, but will provide independent expert evidence on which the level of compensation will be calculated. Be prepared to pay a fee for this; the amount should be included in your compensation claim.

7. Damage to your bicycle. Ask for a free quote from a cycle repair shop. If you can afford it, have the bike repaired and ask for and retain a detailed receipt.

8. Your claim should include losses from damage to clothing and incidental expenses attributable to the incident, such as bus fares.

Remember

Keep all receipts and submit photocopies with your claim. Send your claim and all letters by registered delivery.

Usually the highways department will refuse to admit liability but persistence coupled to threats of legal action will pay off. Note there is a three-year time limit for claims for personal injury and five years for damage to property.

Bikes for disabled people

Bikes are available which are specially suited for people with severe disabilities. Cycling as a therapeutic activity is of great value across a spectrum of disabilities, and it is just as exhilarating, perhaps more so, for disabled cyclists compared with those who are able bodied.

A number of specially designed bikes are available, but the vast majority of people with disabilities can generally ride some sort of bike, tandem or adapted tricycle. Tandems are used a good deal by blind cyclists who ride at the rear. Tricycles are used both for adults and children who have difficulty with balance. Open-framed bicycles, i.e. those with no crossbar, are useful for people with leg mobility problems, as are hand-cranked bikes for those with no leg mobility. Side-by-side tandems, or buddy bikes, have a weird pedal arrangement, but are more suitable for many people. Steering and braking is controlled on one side.

A Duet is a detachable wheelchair, which can be attached to a conventional bicycle to become a tandem and allows someone to go longer distances than would be possible in a normal wheelchair. I tried out a Duet and found it easy to cycle, very safe, and a marvellous way for those confined to wheelchairs to get out and about with a cycling companion. However, Duets cost about £3000, a sum which probably cannot be justified for many people. Fortunately, quite a number of charity and local authority organizations have purchased Duets and the list is growing rapidly. For more information on bicycles which disabled people can use, contact Neatworks, tel. 01890 883456, for up-to-date information. They also can hireout Duets subject to availability.

Essentials checklist

Bike

As you are touring along, listen to your bike. Watch for faults and catch them before they become too serious. Things do work free and need tightening and adjusting.

Water bottle and cage

Repair kit

Essential minimum: three tyre levers, patches and pump. Spare inner tube. Puncture repair kit. Adjustable spanner. Screwdriver. Allen keys. Spoke key. Brake blocks and cables. Some nuts and bolts. Bicycle lights. Cycle lock. Chain splitter. A cool tool is a useful investment.

Remember that preventive maintenance is better than repairing badly maintained bikes in the rain.

Maps and compass

Bike bell

Defined, according to one American magazine, as an audible warning device! Rumour has it that it will be made law, and its use is also more polite than shouting at people.

Mudguards

For wimps, but they save on the laundry bill.

Rear-view mirrors
A good idea, and they add to your safety.

Helmets
Helmets are a difficult and personal decision. But listen to your mother for once. Mine says a helmet makes me look silly. However, in contrast, all the major cycling organizations recommend that you wear a helmet, especially when cycling off-road.

Sunglasses
In Scotland these are more useful for keeping wind, dust and flying creatures out.

Be seen
The argument for all those Day-Glo colours is so that motorists see you and don't squash you. Unfortunately, people giggle uncontrollably when you go into the pub. Waterproofs are vital.

Shoes
I use ordinary cross trainers, with toe clips. However, cycling shoes have firmer soles and are supposedly more efficient and less stressful on the foot.

Midge repellent and first-aid kit

Food
Especially compact, high-energy sources such as sandwiches, chocolate and bananas.

Water
You can get very dehydrated.

Camera and lots of film

Money
Lots and lots – cash, cheques and credit card. Credit cards are accepted to some extent. Banking facilities are limited and Cashlines are the exception, not the rule. There is little risk of having money or property stolen in the islands. I routinely leave my bike unlocked. Honesty boxes are an indication that you shouldn't be unduly paranoid about not carrying cash – which isn't an invitation to be unduly careless. But it is a shame to waste valuable holiday time trying to find a bank.

MOUNTAIN BIKING

Mountain biking has great popular appeal and has encouraged more and more people to get out into the fresh air. But people have done a fair bit of off-road cycling and mountain biking over the years prior to the invention of the off-road bike. So what is the difference? Where do the real hard men of mountain biking go? How do you recognize them? Sure, that's them with the brown strip of mud up their backs!

Cycling is split into subcultures, with road racers looking down on tourers, and tourers looking down on mountain bikes, and mountain bikers not giving a damn – they just want to get on with having a good blast around in the fresh air. I made my first sighting of a genuine mountain biker in a country park where mountain biking is meant to be organized, but where I was to have my first taste of wild jungle cycling. I warn you that if you get a bit of a taste for this mountain bike lark you get seriously muddy, brambled and sweaty, while leaping about on the bike as if it were a pogo stick. Purists are known to cycle down stairs and skill levels are remarkably high, so don't follow them or you will end up in Casualty.

If you want to get completely involved and go mountain bike racing, there are events all over Scotland. They advertise in mountain bike magazines, and it is also a good idea to seek out clubs of enthusiasts. The best source of information on clubs is *Mountain Bike UK*, or ask at cycle shops, particularly the specialists dealing with mountain bikes.

Club cycling is very enjoyable and joining a bunch of like-minded people is good for getting information. Mountain biking is an activity which should be undertaken with companions, for safety as well as for sociability, and also to get you to push yourself a bit more if you are inclined to sloth. However, that can go too far and sometimes groups are pretty competitive, which can be off-putting. And serious mountain bike racers do get hurt. For them, helmets are essential.

If you are going to buy a bike, though, should it be a mountain bike? In my opinion, not necessarily. The orgy of consumerism which attends mountain bikes and mountain biking seems a bit weird. Bike shops love mountain bikes because they have rejuvenated the cycle trade and any way of keeping bike shops in business is good news. People who used to inhabit bike shops were generally flat-capped and clad in moleskin breeches. Bikes had a working class, utilitarian image and needed a major shot in the arm from the marketing men. Mountain bikes appeared, emblazoned with 'psycho-active' paintjobs, to say nothing of the green image and healthy lifestyle.

Suddenly bikes are fashion items, to be hung on the back of smart cars along with the surfboard or the skis. The bike shops find themselves frequented – nay, overrun – by young trendies with bulging wallets eager to buy the latest titanium components. These are bikes that you decorate your car or your body with. Mountain bikes are high street jewellery to be worn with aggressive self-assurance like gold medallions.

The image of the bike as working class runs deep in our culture and has caused the bike to be rejected. Norman Tebbit's 'on your bike' is full of disdain, despite the fact that many cycle shops have called themselves that. It is therefore interesting that the ordinary bike is out of fashion, and that the vogue is for Day-Glo mountain bikes slung on the backs of cars as an extension of car culture. It doesn't seem to matter that these are no better for almost all uses than road bikes. It doesn't matter that people hiring bikes just get baffled by 21 gears. Or that no thief bothers to nick ordinary road bikes anymore, when there are all these brightly paint-jobbed things instead.

Sadly, there is a growing tension between (normally) middle-aged walkers out to enjoy a stroll after Sunday lunch, and young peat-churning tearaways who have hip-hop music hot-wired into their brains. Part of the problem is that mountain bikers look so awful, in their bright Lycra outfits. The other is that bikes are so silent and fast that they do genuinely scare people out walking. The source of the problem is that by and large the walkers are middle-aged adults and the bikers are lanky kids, doing what lanky kids do best – upsetting adults.

In fact, the conflict between walkers and cyclists is not as serious in Scotland as it is in England, but as cyclists are banned from certain areas in England, and come to Scotland instead, it has the potential to become a real concern. There is no excuse for cyclists to be bad-mannered to walkers. Just as cyclists don't like being intimidated by cars, there is no reason why walkers should put up with cyclists behaving like zombies. The hypocrisy of cyclists who are furious and indignant at inconsiderate car drivers but inflict the same treatment on innocent walkers is obvious to all but the individuals concerned, and gives mountain bikers a bad name. This is rather sad, as walkers and cyclists are on the same side in wanting to maintain access to the land and the conflict between them gives the landowners an opportunity to restrict access further.

Mountain biking developed in California in the 1970s as part of the sport as mind-altering substance, freethinking lifestyle of the west coast. People started taking pick-ups crammed with roadster bikes into the mountains and battering at full tilt down forest tracks. One only has to read the mountain bike magazines to see where the problems arise – it is devastatingly simple. Mountain biking is all about thrills and spills, and has little to do with quiet appreciation of the countryside.

Scotland has large tracts of country which are not only suitable for mountain bikes, but are almost made for it. The massive estates owned by the Forestry Commission have been completely opened up and there are many hill roads all over the Scottish mountains which are accessible to bikes. As a cyclist you do have access rights to the Scottish hills, provided you act considerately and sensibly. But do be cautious. Bikes cover long distances remarkably quickly, and it is easy to get lost or in trouble unless you have proper bike tools and sensible clothing and maps. Scotland's hills can be dangerous unless they are treated with respect.

The issue of access is an interesting one. What follows is my opinion, and while I think it is accurate I take no responsibility for the use made of it. In Scotland there is no criminal law of trespass as there is in England and Wales. Instead, trespass is covered by civil law, which in practice means that unless you are doing wheelies on someone's flowerbeds there is very little they can do. Legally, bicycles are not vehicles and you have essentially the same right to roam as that which walkers enjoy. However, it is fair to say that this is an untested area of Scottish law. The landowner could have injunctions taken out against individuals to prevent trespass but that is going to get a bit tiresome if he has to do it for everyone with a bike. Whatever one might feel about the politics of landownership, the importance of keeping up friendly relations with estate workers cannot be stressed enough. Most people are friendly and helpful and it is well worth calling in at estate offices, chatting to keepers you may meet or telephoning ahead to say what you are planning to do. In many of the key areas for mountain biking, such as Royal Deeside, the Cairngorms, the Grampians and the Borders, local bike shops and estates have agreed access. Some of the shops consider themselves to be access officers, which seems a bit presumptuous, but they are worth talking to for up-to-date information. Information on estates is available in *Heading for the Scottish Hills*, published jointly by the Scottish Landowners Federation and the Mountaineering Council of Scotland.

If you get chatting to people on the hill, you'll find out where the pub is, or if there are any bothies nearby, or other interesting facts that you might not know. If estates are shooting in one area, or have a reason for asking you to avoid the area at a specific time it is best to keep clear or you may get shot. But landowners can be rather mischievous about using the stalking season or lambing to restrict access much more generally than is reasonable. Legally you are OK as long as you act reasonably and are doing no damage to property. Always shut gates, and bear in mind that it is the stalkers and estate workers who will have to repair any damage you cause.

In short, it is in everyone's interest if cyclists can stay on good terms with other users of the countryside, and in that way restrictions on access will be avoided.

LONG-DISTANCE ROUTES

Various initiatives are under way to improve cycle route provision in Scotland. More information on these routes and other, shorter, routes nearby is given in the indicated chapters. At present the following routes exist:

Tweed Valley Cycle Route (see Chapter 9)

This route is signposted from Biggar to Berwick-upon-Tweed and follows the River Tweed. Problems of logistics make it hard to do in practice, but it is a good idea. A leaflet is available from Scottish Tourist Board, 22 Ravelston Terrace, Edinburgh, tel. 0131 332-2433, or Jedburgh Tourist Information Office, tel. 01835 863435.

Spey Valley Cycle Route (see Chapter 7)

A good scheme which encourages people to explore the Spey Valley by bicycle. Leaflets are available from Aviemore Tourist Information Office, Grampian Road, tel. 01479 810363, or Elgin Tourist Information Office, 17 High Street, tel. 01343 542666.

Sustrans National Routes

Some sections are already complete and there are plans for routes from Carlisle, Dumfries, Ayr and Glasgow to Inverness. The project has been partially funded by a large grant from the Lottery Millennium Fund, so progress should be rapid. Sustrans is a charity lobbying for and building cycle tracks, and will provide details of existing and planned routes. They request you send a SAE for details and appreciate donations at 53 Cochrane Street, Glasgow, tel. 0141 552-8241.

British Waterways Board

Forth & Clyde Canal/Union Canal from Glasgow to Edinburgh (see Chapter 11)
For more information, contact British Waterways Board, Canal House, Applecross Street, Glasgow G4, tel. 0141 332-6936.

Great Glen Cycle Route (see Chapter 5)

The Forestry Commission provides many routes through its forests and publishes leaflets with up-to-date information. Contact Forestry Enterprise, Fort William, tel. 01397 702184. The Forestry Commission is split into areas. Either contact local Tourist Information Offices, or the head office of the Forestry Commission at 231 Corstorphine Road, Edinburgh, tel. 0131 334-0303, for more details.

Scottish Office Trunk Road Initiative

The Scottish Office is paying some heed to the needs of cyclists by supporting Sustrans and building a dedicated cycle route next to the A74(M) north from Gretna, and attempting to provide safe cycle routes adjacent to new trunk roads. It is worth lobbying and expressing your desire for better and safer traffic-free cycle facilities, and addressing them to The Cycling Initiative, The Scottish Office, New St Andrew's House, Leith, Edinburgh, to get the rhetoric converted into action.

Scottish Tourist Board, 23 Ravelston Terrace, Edinburgh, EH4 3EU, tel. 0131 332-2433.

Caledonian Macbrayne, Ferry Terminal, Gourock, tel. 01475 650100 (enquiries)/0990 650000 (bookings).

P&O Scottish Ferries, Jamieson's Quay, Aberdeen, AB9 8DL, tel. 01224 572615.

ScotRail, 58 Port Dundas Road, Glasgow, G4 0HG.

Cycle Touring Club, Cotterell House, 69 Meadrow, Godalming, Surrey, GU7 3HS, tel. 01483 417217.

CTC Scotland. Contact Drew Moyes, 24 Newbridge Street, Ayr, KA7 1JX, tel. 01292 285313.

Scottish Youth Hostels Association, National Office, 7 Glebe Crescent, Stirling, FK8 2JA, tel. 01786 451181.

For a list of **Scottish Independent Hostels**, send an SAE to Pete Thomas, Croft Bunkhouse, Portnalong, Isle of Skye, IV47 8SL.

BIBLIOGRAPHY

Books are heavy and when you are cycling you cannot carry stacks of them. However, the following are recommended:

Pocket Reference Scotland, Hilary Macartney (HarperCollins).
A thorough gazetteer for the whole of the country, plus a number of extensive motoring excursions and historical background information.

Scotland the Best, Peter Irvine (Mainstream).
Accessible and well-researched personal guide to the very best of Scotland.
Cycle Touring Club Handbook, available to CTC members.

SELECTIVE INDEX OF PLACE NAMES

INDEX

COLLINS

Other cycling titles published by HarperCollins Publishers:

Bartholomew Cycling in the Cotswolds

Bartholomew Cycling in the South Downs

In each guide there are 30 cycle tours, ranging from short rides suitable for all the family, to half- and full-day rides for the more experienced and adventurous, rounding off with a *grande randonnée* – a 100 mile route round each area.

Covering on- and off-road routes, each tour has concise, easy-to-follow directions and uses specially created mapping at around 1.5 miles to 1 inch. A separate box gives succinct information for each tour, including how to get there, total mileage, ascents and descents, and a description of the terrain. Places to visit along the way, refreshment stops and picnic sites are also listed.

Each guide is endorsed by the Cyclists' Touring Club

£8.99 each

COLLINS POCKET REFERENCE

*Other Pocket Reference titles published by
HarperCollins Publishers:*

Card Games £4.99

❖

Etiquette £4.99

❖

Finding a Job £4.99

❖

First Names £4.99

❖

Letter Writing £4.99

❖

Quotations £4.99

❖

Ready Reference £4.99

❖

Selling your Home £4.99

❖

Starting your own Business £4.99

Available from all good bookshops

COLLINS